T0330696

Making a Difference in Marketing

Establishing a difference is the lynchpin of marketing. It can be achieved in many ways. The results can be magical and powerful: such as increasing, with little expense, the price of a little regarded fish from £0.15 a kilo to £1.00. As with many other disciplines which have great value, this potency has often resulted in the discussion of marketing being prey to increasing complexity. This frequently intimidates those marketing could help. Often it is due to the touting of supposedly new paradigms, given plausibility by conveniently invented metrics, and an emphasis on the rational and conscious over the emotional and unconscious, despite the latter aspects appearing to be the basis for much choice.

This imbalance has been highlighted by recent insights from psychology, neurology and behavioural economics. Rather than simply embracing these advances, the focus of marketing has been on additional layers of intricacy and a weighting of emphasis towards means of communication, further distancing marketing from its base.

This book aims to cut through to the pivotal role of differentiation, illustrated by case histories and the advances in the related fields referred to, particularly the work of psychologists such as Daniel Kahneman. Unlike much writing on marketing, it has tried to follow Einstein's advice to be "as simple as possible, but no simpler".

Jonathan Cahill has had extensive experience in advertising, research and marketing, and successfully developed and marketed his own brand. He has previously written *Igniting the Brand: Strategies Which Shot Brands to Success* and *Marketing Rethink: Reassessing the Roots, Practice and Diversions of Marketing*. Jonathan provides consultancy through his company Z Limited, as well as articles which have been published in the UK and Australia on the marketing of wine. He is currently a lecturer in marketing at the Westminster Business School.

"A wonderfully spikey read about who has got it right and who has got it wrong when it comes to understanding how to build a brand. Cahill takes you back to basics to explain why in each and every case he uses. An enjoyable, easy read that will stay with me." *Tessa Gooding, IPA Director of Communications, UK*

"*Making a Difference in Marketing* offers a refreshing approach of going back to the Basics. Insightful, intellectually entertaining and containing a vast number of rich, inspiring quotes and references, worth exploring on their own. This book is a worthwhile and informative read for anyone with personal or professional interest in the Marketing profession." *Christian Ohm, Head of Consumer & Market Intelligence Europe, Mazda Motor Europe*

Making a Difference in Marketing

The Foundation of Competitive Advantage

Jonathan Cahill

Routledge
Taylor & Francis Group

LONDON AND NEW YORK

First published 2017
by Routledge
2 Park Square, Milton Park, Abingdon, Oxon OX14 4RN

and by Routledge
711 Third Avenue, New York, NY 10017

Routledge is an imprint of the Taylor & Francis Group, an informa business

© 2017 Jonathan Cahill

British Library Cataloguing-in-Publication Data
A catalogue record for this book is available from the British Library

Library of Congress Cataloging-in-Publication Data
A catalog record for this book has been requested

ISBN: 978-1-138-03685-7 (hbk)
ISBN: 978-1-315-17825-7 (ebk)

Typeset in Times New Roman
by Apex CoVantage, LLC

Contents

Introduction

As one of the greatest writers on marketing, Theodore Levitt, put it, "consumers are unpredictable, varied, fickle, stupid, short-sighted, stubborn and generally bothersome."[1] Despite this unpromising material, some of the solutions marketing provides are almost magical. But the human element always needs to be borne in mind, as physician Sir William Osler observed: "if all patients were the same, then medicine would be a science and not an art." Unfortunately this basic truth is often lost sight of in marketing. Despite the repeated attempts to make marketing conform to the more mechanistic and deductive approaches of a natural science, it needs to be remembered that, given its subject matter is people, it is a social science. It is for this reason that this book has tried to fully consider the wider human context which is the broad canvas of marketing, rather than the narrower marketing silo which often limits a more holistic approach. Many observations are presented which are not usually associated with marketing but have direct relevance, as they help give insights into the way we behave and so inform a consideration of marketing in the real world.

In terms of the stage which the discussion of marketing has reached, it has ostensibly become increasingly sophisticated. But this has resulted in going far beyond the roots of the practice and has ended up playing in the branches, constructing evermore complex intellectual tree houses which have little to do with what actually happens on the ground. There is also an inherent danger in this detachment from the basics, as it is susceptible to an outlook described by Duncan J. Watts where "we think we have understood things that in fact we have simply papered over with a plausible sounding story."[2] What are constructed are a series of what critic Stephen Jay Gould, in another context, described as "Just So Stories" which may sound good, but whether they are true or not remains unknown.[3] Above all it suffers from the toxic danger described by Nobel Prize winner Barry Marshall when he quoted the historian Daniel Boorstin in his acceptance speech: "the greatest obstacle to knowledge is not ignorance: it is the illusion of knowledge."[4]

Nevertheless this playing in the branches is great fun, because it means that those involved can make portentous statements without any solid foundations other than the coherence of their story which, as Daniel Kahneman observed, is all that is necessary for something to be believed, even if it is untrue. Reinforcing this is consensual validation when, as Eric Fromm explained, "it is naively assumed that the fact that the majority of people share certain ideas or feelings proves the validity of these ideas and feelings."[5] He noted that "we know that people can maintain an unshakeable faith in any proposition, however absurd, when they are sustained by a community of like-minded believers."[6] The important point is to break away from this and to think differently. This is well demonstrated by Neil Woodford, one of the most successful fund managers in the UK, who purposely avoids what he describes as the "crowded consensus"[7] of the city of London by having his office well outside of London, up the Thames in Henley.

Unfortunately the Socratic mantra of "a life unexamined is a life not worth living" is not often taken to heart in marketing. No more so is this true than in academic papers on the subject. This was highlighted by J. Scott Armstrong, professor of marketing at Wharton Business School.[8] He remarked on the difficulty of finding constructive papers, estimating that fewer than two per cent of those published in leading academic journals were useful. Yet the academic establishment has a self-regarding obsession with such papers. Richard Thaler, one of the principal founders of behavioural economics, pointed out that at the University of Chicago's Booth School of Business, you were "only as good as your last paper".[9] It would be more constructive if the predominant criterion was the clarity of understanding of the subject given to the students, rather than an apparent obsession with academic preening.

This is not to say that students are eager to think. Dan Ariely is professor of Behavioural Economics at Duke University. When he taught an MBA course at Harvard Business School, he told his class that all the models and theories could be found in the textbooks and that he would explore marketing in his lectures. By half-term the feedback from his students was one of the worst he had ever received. Their main complaint was that he had not given them any framework. These individuals were top businessmen – otherwise many would not have been sent, at great cost, to the course by their companies – yet even they needed a surrogate for thought.

But this attitude extends to a widespread approach. As James Surowiecki observed:

> it's much easier to follow the strategy which seems rational rather than the strategy which is rational. As a result, managers anxious to protect their jobs come to mimic each other. In doing so they destroy whatever

information advantage they might have had, since the mimicking managers are not really relying on their own information but are relying on the information of others.[10]

They sacrifice the differentiation that their own independent thought might bring. This is also mirrored by those who practice marketing. As Levitt pointed out, in response to the question,

"What's new?" . . . Those who answer professionally, with neatly engineered formulas, elegant strategic paradigms and finely honed analytical techniques are sure to get an audience in this world of great uncertainty, profound ambiguity and intense competition. Thus the ubiquity of the shaman in business dress.[11]

This is even more evident now than in Levitt's day, as the intervening years have tended to add yet further layers to the Gordian Knot which they purport to unravel but which they only add to. Margaret Heffernan described it well when she observed that "like Daedalus, we build labyrinths of such cunning complexity that we cannot find our way out. And we are blind to the blindness these complex structures necessarily confer. So we forget all about it."[12] After all, the more complex the situation which is engineered, the greater the opportunity for the self-proclaimed expert.

In addition there is what psychologist Robert Zajonc called "the mere exposure effect", whereby the repetition of an arbitrary stimulus can eventually create a mild affection for it among people. He found in an experiment that Turkish or Turkish-sounding words which were presented more often were subsequently rated much more favourably than words which had been shown only once or twice. He argued that the effect of repetition on liking is a profoundly important biological fact which extends to all animals.[13] This can have an effect on the establishment of beliefs as well as being an aid in the differentiation of brands.

There is a rather prosaic aphorism of which few in the world of marketing seem to be aware: if it walks like a duck, if it swims like a duck and if it quacks like a duck, then it's a duck. Unfortunately many allow these canards to roam free and fail to realise that they need to be thoroughly cooked. J. Scott Armstrong put such approaches into perspective with his "seer-sucker theory": "no matter how much evidence exists that seers do not exist, suckers will pay for the existence of seers."[14] The danger of reliance on the expert is illustrated by compelling research which shows that, in the presence of experts, people delegate the consideration of an issue to them. In brain scan research,[15] when respondents were asked to make choices on their own, there was a sudden jump in activity in those areas of the brain associated with evaluating options. But when they received expert advice on these options, they followed that advice and appeared to do so with no thought as to the inherent merits of the options. The evaluating areas of their brains flatlined. Rather than using the expert to help inform their choice, they appeared to have delegated it to them – their thinking had gone AWOL.

Such a climate has cultivated many propositions which, delivered with great conviction, are nevertheless of little practical use. One such is the supposed requirement that a brand should have a "brand purpose". Although sympathy needs to be extended to a brand suffering from the existential angst of not having a purpose, this, like so many other approaches, treats the relationship between a brand and its consumers as one which takes place in a vacuum, reminiscent of the economist's trope of "everything else being equal". Clearly it isn't the case, and a brand exists in a dynamic situation where there are many other factors at play, not all of which are easily identified and certainly not capable of being addressed in isolation. Most of these result from the particular context in which a brand operates – competition. Like everything else, a brand is defined by its context. If one is to talk about purpose, then the concept of a brand would have little purpose if there was no competition. Indeed one of the chief roles of a brand is not to be a lone island but rather to be a tree which stands out from the forest. This is achieved by differentiation, which taps into the essence of its being.

The importance of context is paramount in any consideration, as the American philosopher, John Dewey, observed: "the most pervasive fallacy of philosophic thinking goes back to neglect of context."[16] Today, behavioural economists recognise that people are susceptible to irrelevant influences from their immediate environment. Failure to acknowledge this can lead to what is called the Fundamental Attribution Error, whereby people tend to fixate on supposedly stable character traits and overlook the influence of context. This is profound, as Steve Martin and his colleagues stated, "it is not information per se that leads people to make decisions, but the context in which that information is presented."[17] They went on to add that "as the amount of information we have to make better decisions increases, the less likely we are to use that information when we have to decide. We are just as likely to be influenced by small changes."[18] Similarly the points of differentiation can often appear small and even inconsequential, but this does not detract from their potency, as will become evident. Ironically, many of these differences which appear to have contributed to marketing success are often not overtly competitive. This has been the case with the enduring success of Jack Daniel's, whose advertising merely featured the context of the brand in terms of where it was produced and never directly talked about the brand itself.

Definitions: the essential foundations

In marketing, the roots of much obscurity have been created by so-called definitions which, on closer inspection, reveal themselves to be no such thing. The American Marketing Association puts forward a definition for marketing as "the activity, set of institutions, and processes for creating, communicating, delivering, and exchanging offerings that have value for customers, clients, partners, and society at large". This gobbledygook contributes little other than confusion and is not even a definition, in the sense of expressing the essence of a concept. Rather it is merely a description which serves little purpose other than window-dressing and, more probably, the consensual compromise that it so often the outcome of a committee. It is disturbing that this organisation does not appear to have any firm grasp of a concept which is so fundamental to it and the field it represents.

To consider any subject there must be an agreed understanding of what it means – which is why there are dictionaries. Without this, all discussion is based on a foundation of sand, as neither party has a solid, agreed basis for what they are talking about. The lack of a clear definition for marketing runs this risk, as those who practice it feel they know what it is, but with the application of a little rigour, this supposed understanding evaporates. Such a situation smacks of what John Locke described as "an unpardonable negligence" when they "familiarly use words which the propriety of language has affixed to very important ideas, without any distinct meaning at all".[19] He described the unsteady application of words as a perfect abuse of language which is either a "great folly or greater dishonesty".

Words are the currency of thought, and if there is nothing behind a word, then it is has no more use than a score in Scrabble. As John Locke wrote, "they remain empty sounds, with little or no significance amongst those who think it enough to have them often in their mouth . . . without troubling their heads to examine what are the precise ideas they stand for." He went on to comment on the affected obscurity that resulted, which was "like a mist before people's eyes" and, when they talk about it, "fills their discourse with abundance of empty unintelligible noise and jargon . . . the apter to produce wonder because they could not be understood." He noted that they found it strange if they were questioned as to the meaning of their terms. Such is often the case when people in marketing are asked to define it; frequently an air of incomprehension arises and the response is often garbled and tends to take shelter in a mantra they recite without any real understanding as to its meaning – if indeed it has one.

There are other so-called definitions of marketing which are trotted out, often with little realisation as to how hollow they are. One standard cliché is that it involves meeting consumer needs. But this is more the province of new product development than marketing. As mentioned previously, the root is competition, so it seems only appropriate that this be part of the definition of marketing. A hopefully more grounded definition is "the achievement of competitive advantage through meaningful differentiation, in terms of product or perceptions, and the exploitation of this to the full". This appears to be the essence of the subject. There may be other definitions which are more appropriate, but they do not appear to have declared themselves.

In this definition, differentiation is clearly pivotal. Admittedly it is often recognised when assessing marketing, but it is generally revealed as the discovery of a failing rather than the essential foundation for any marketing consideration. It should be a key point of departure rather than something which is only recognised with hindsight. Two research companies in the United States teamed up to do a study of how well brands were differentiated in a diverse set of categories.[20] They looked at forty-six product/service categories and found that the leading brands in forty of these were becoming less differentiated in the minds of consumers. In four of the remaining six categories the leading brands were perceived as maintaining their level of differentiation, and only two were regarded as becoming more differentiated. In support of this, a study by Ernst and Young of new brands showed that around 80 per cent failed. The primary reason cited for failure was lack of differentiation. The absence of differentiation forces brands to compete on the basis of factors such as price, which undermines the reasons why brands exist in the first place.

Advertising Age is one of the most prominent publications on marketing, yet they view any consideration of its definition as "too educational/academic". The logical consequence of this could be an unintended endorsement of a situation where people don't really know what they are talking about – never a firm basis for discussion or, more importantly, action.

The consequence is that intellectual ghettoes are created where intense discussion takes place on subjects which appear plausible and around which a theoretical framework has been built such that it is this which is debated rather than the issue at hand being addressed. A prime example of this is the diagrams which proliferate and which purport to be guides to the cognitive processing of an issue but which end up with the user trying to identify each of the components rather than arriving at the result to which they are supposed to lead. As Montaigne observed, "it is more of a job to interpret the interpretations than to interpret the things and there are more books about books than about any other subject." The outcome is that everyone feels enlightened, although they have shed little light.

Hopefully this book is in tune with the spirit of Bruce Springsteen on the occasion of his first performance in the UK. He was angered by the hype around the show with posters announcing "FINALLY! London is ready for Bruce Springsteen". He destroyed the posters and flyers, saying, "my business is SHOW business, not TELLING. You show people and let them decide."[21] This is not as disinterested as it sounds, because when the audience decides of their own accord, then the message has far more potency than if they are told – a basic truth of human behaviour and thus of marketing.

Given this situation, the role of this book is to try to increase the focus on the crucial role that differentiation plays in marketing and the vital edge it gives in the competition, which is the nature of any market. Failing to take this into account leaves the brand susceptible to the siren call of external factors, such as price promotion, and moves it further into the world of commodities where its description as a brand becomes only a label and not a reality. Differentiation is at the root of many great marketing successes, but its potency should not obscure the elegance of some of the solutions it provides. Usually the understanding of where differentiation can be applied tends to be limited in its scope, whereas there is often a wide panorama of choice. Because such outcomes are so powerful, there is often a tendency to overlook how a simple concept which differentiates can resonate with the consumer and so effect great change. This is part of the magic of marketing.

1   Context

The foundation of differentiation

Much emphasis has been put on the importance of a proper consideration of the context in which a brand operates. This is not always a given; there is always the possibility of engineering the context in order to produce a situation in which differentiation can thrive. Sometimes this can be achieved by constructing simple choice options. As Noah Goldstein and Steve Martin pointed out in *The Small BIG*, "it is not information per se that leads people to make decisions, but the context in which that information is presented."[22] An example was provided by Wayne Viner, an English ice cream salesman, who noted that, "if you look them in the eye and ask 'small, medium or large', 90 per cent of adults will go for the medium."[23] This is known as the Compromise Effect, whereby we avoid extremes and take the middle course.

The fundamental influence of context was shown by studies of rats. When a rat was conditioned by associating a sound with a shock, the rat became afraid not only of the sound but also of the box in which the conditioning took place – the context of the sound.[24] Also if hungry rats are given food in one compartment of two chambers, they will later spend more time in that compartment. On a wider platform Daniela Kaufer and Darlene Francis (at the University of California, Berkeley) did extensive research on the nature-nurture relationship and concluded that "environments can be as deterministic as we once believed only genes could be."[25]

Context frames the situation and also gives the basis for differentiation. This was the essence of Charles Darwin's theory of natural selection, as it was based on a process he referred to as "descent with modification". It involved focusing on individual animals. A particular example he provided includes finches on the Galapagos Islands, which were different, as they possessed advantages suited to the particular environment in which they had to survive. Darwin realised that the variability allowing adaptation was already present in the Finch population. Nature did not "produce" the variation within the Finch population; it already existed. Rather, nature "selected" from these inherent traits those that best fostered survival and reproduction, and it was this choosing which Darwin called "natural selection". As he summed it up, "it is not the strongest of the species that survive, nor the most intelligent, but the one most responsive to change". Consequently the process he described involved a keen awareness of the requirements of survival in the particular environment and the choice of those inherent differences which best served this. Similarly a brand's acute understanding of its context and its own intrinsic attributes which it selects in response to this give it the best chance of prospering in its environment of the market.

At the most fundamental level, the brand needs to realise that the context it is in is a market. EasyJet is a very successful budget airline which has made many winning initiatives, yet its marketing does not appear to be fully informed by its position in the UK. It has a market share of around 20 per cent of passengers.[26] Yet in its advertising it promotes the generic benefits of air travel to Europe in a very creative and attractive way. This would be fine if their share was over half the market and they wanted to grow the overall market, but it is difficult to see its direct relevance when presenting a competitive advantage which is a more pertinent goal for a company with only about a fifth of the market. Their group commercial director stated that a new campaign promoting going to Europe by plane was to "lead customers through [these] difficult times" and went on to talk about the uncertainty brought about Brexit and perceptions of terrorism: "While it is challenging, consumers don't need to change their behaviour. They still need to see their families, go on business trips or go on holiday. The [new Why Not?] campaign was a deliberate feel-good act demonstrating our brand values and benefits."[27] This statement turned rather curious when the values and benefits shown were not those of the brand but rather the generic ones provided by air travel. This might well persuade viewers to fly, but why with EasyJet? Surely "brand values and benefits" need to be particular to the brand; otherwise they are just "industry values and benefits" which give little traction for the individual brand. Unfortunately this is yet another example of the familiar conceit that when something is framed in terms of brands, it confers validity even when, with a little touch of rigour, it evaporates.

The physical environment can play a role in differentiation with consumers, as well as with the rats mentioned previously. This was evident in a study of selling wine in a supermarket. Four German and four French wines, which were matched for price and dryness, were put on shelves in an English supermarket. German and French music was then played on alternate days. On days when the German music was played, 73 per cent of the wine bought was German, while on the days of French music, 77 per cent of the wine purchased was French. Yet, when asked whether the music has influenced their choice, only one shopper in seven said it had.[28]

The importance of context in terms of a restaurant was highlighted by Jeremy King, one of the most successful restaurateurs in London, with restaurants such as the Ivy, Le Caprice, the Wolseley and a raft of other successes. He commented that

> a lot of the success of a restaurant is due to the feel of the place. We never attempt to impose an idea on a building – it tells us what to do. I'd like to create a contemporary restaurant. But I've never stood in a contemporary building that did it for me.[29]

Inventing a context

Perceptual contrast is a basic concept in psychology. This is the idea that a person's perception of an offer can be changed not by changing the offer itself, but by changing the context in which the offer is presented. A £32 bottle of wine seems expensive if it appears halfway down a list, at the bottom of which is the house wine at £15. But £32 will appear to be a more reasonable price if a small change is made by putting a more expensive wine, around £50, first on the list.

This was expanded on by Dan Ariely in his example of an *Economist* subscription offer.[30] Three options were given: an Internet-only subscription at $59, a print-only option at $125 and a print-and-Internet option at $125. Ariely observed that a decision between just two options of Internet-only and print-only would have taken a bit of thinking, and "thinking is difficult and sometimes unpleasant". So, by providing three options, the *Economist* offered a no-brainer: next to the print-only, the print-and-Internet option appeared to be a much better option. In effect, this was a ruse for achieving their overall goal of selling the printed version of the magazine by changing the context in which the option was presented.

Ariely put this offer to one hundred students at MIT's Sloan School of Management. Only sixteen went for the Internet-only option, none for the print-only and eighty-four for the print-and-Internet. But when the print-only option, which he accurately referred to as the decoy, was removed, then only thirty-two students chose the print-and-Internet and sixty-eight chose the Internet-only option. On this Ariely commented: "most people don't know what they want unless they see it in context. We don't know what kind of bike we want – until we see a champ in the Tour de France ratcheting the gears on a particular model."

Another example of the decoy effect was when Williams-Sonoma, an upmarket kitchen shop in the United States, introduced a home bread baking machine for $275. Most customers were not interested. A marketing research firm suggested that a possible solution to this would be to add an additional model which was larger and with a price 50 per cent higher. Sales of the original model began to rise. The introduction of the second machine meant that the original one now had something against which to differentiate itself, to its advantage.[31] This is the anchoring effect and can often be used to change the context of a situation in which a brand operates and give greater scope for its differentiation. Another familiar use of this tactic is on a menu when a more expensive dish is featured to help pull choice up to those in the second tier of prices.

Another approach involving context was in the choice offered when buying billiard tables. There were two tables, priced at $320 and $3,000. In the first week, customers were shown the lower-priced table and encouraged to trade up. The averaged amount paid was $500. Then, in the second week, they were led to the $3,000 table, regardless of what they wanted to see. With this approach the average sale rose to $1,000.[32]

In terms of changing the whole context, Starbucks was a master. Rather than trying to compete with other places selling coffee, it invented a whole new category of coffee shops and coffee language. Some of this had derived from a visit the eventual CEO, Howard Schultz, had made to Italy to investigate the coffee culture there. Rather than trying to compete with other places selling coffee, they invented a whole new category of coffee shops. One of the prizes Schultz brought back was a whole new vocabulary of coffee, such as "espresso", "latte", "macchiato", and so on, which immediately set Starbucks apart from most coffee, which at that time in the United States was largely filter coffee.

The coffee ambience at Starbucks was made to look upscale. They did everything they could to make the experience feel different from other places selling coffee in more prosaic surroundings, such as Dunkin' Donuts. This enabled them to forget the pricing territory on which such potential competitors operated by defining a completely new area where the prices of coffee at Dunkin' Donuts were no longer relevant, as it was on another planet. In 2008 Schultz took back control of Starbucks when it was faltering. One of the areas he focused on was to inject a little more "theatre" into the coffee-making experience, retraining the baristas to improve the service. Starbucks shares rose 52 per cent in one year.[33] Part of their projected expertise was also built up by the vast range of offerings; in the UK the Future Foundation found that with 6,000 combinations, if a different drink was ordered each day, it would take 17 years to work through the full range of offerings.[34]

Another approach is to invent a comparison in which the brand can differentiate itself, even though it is not directly comparable. In the UK the ibuprofen brand Nurofen positions itself as being more effective than paracetomol, which it is. But no mention is made of unbranded generic ibuprofen, which is the same product but at around a sixth the price of Nurofen. So a price premium is underwritten by a point of differentiation which is valid but irrelevant.

On a wider scale, context can be changed by altering the framework in which the brand is presented. Even the tone in which it is presented can be of influence. When people receive negative feedback in a warm atmosphere, they leave feeling positive. But when they get positive reviews in a cold and distant tone of voice, they end up feeling bad, despite the good news.[35]

Overall what is known as the framing effect has been shown to be effective, as it is a mental shortcut. Fiske and Taylor[36] felt that humans are, by nature, "cognitive misers", meaning that they prefer to do as little thinking as possible, and frames provide quick and easy ways to process information. Rather than rationally and objectively evaluating new information, the cognitive miser assigns new information to categories that are easy to process mentally. These categories arise from prior information, including schemas, scripts and other knowledge structures, which have been stored in memory and do not require much cognitive energy. The cognitive miser thus tends not to stray far from his or her established beliefs when considering new information. So framers have the power to influence how receivers will interpret messages.

Apple profited by attention to the framework when it went against accepted industry practice and opened its own retail outlets. As computers were an infrequent purchase, it was felt that they did not need to be in convenient locations and so were usually in out-of-town retail sites. One major retailer, Gateway, had about 250 visitors a week. Given that most computers were fairly generic, Steve Jobs, recognising the importance of differentiation, felt that "unless we could find ways to get our message to customers at the store, we were screwed." This thought was further developed by Ron Johnson, the head of the retail division, when he expressed the view that "the store will become the most powerful physical expression of our brand."[37] He had been inspired by the differentiation provided by Ralph Lauren's stores, noting that "whenever I buy a Polo shirt, I think of that mansion which was a physical expression of Ralph's ideal." The building he was referring to was Lauren's wood-panelled, art-filled mansion-like store on 72nd and Madison in New York. This distinctive approach is something which is echoed in other Lauren stores. The one in Milan boasts walls covered with pictures of the Prince of Wales riding in the 1920s and the coat of arms of British families, creating a world of which Lauren's clothes are the natural extension, despite the fact that they are American and not British. This is a neat example of cultural hijacking. The attention to detail in the Apple stores was demonstrated by the fact that Jobs had noticed the sandstone used on the sidewalks when visiting Florence and insisted that this be imported from Italy at ten times the price of a concrete replica.

In marked contrast to the 250 visitors Gateway attracted, Apple's iconic store in the centre of New York, next to Central Park on Fifth Avenue, attracted fifty thousand a week in 2006, its first year. By 2011 Apple recorded sales per square foot of $5,647, the highest of any retailer in the United States. Second was Tiffany & Co, the premium jewellery firm, which delivered $3,085, just over half that of Apple.[38] In certain respects the Apple stores had become temples at whose doors its acolytes would form large queues whenever a new model was released. This inevitably helped give greater status to what resided in this holy of holies.

Apple also gave an example of how the context itself can be used as differentiation when it adopted Intel chips but refused to use the standard payoff line of "Intel inside". Instead Steve Jobs approved a description of the change:

> The Intel Chip. For years it's been trapped inside PCs, inside dull little boxes, dutifully doing dull little tasks, when it could have done so much more. Starting today, the Intel chip will be set free and get to live inside a Mac. Imagine the possibilities.

Ingeniously this turned what was normally presented as a story about having an Intel chip into how the Mac itself could differentiate them.

If everything is considered from the same rational standpoint, there is the danger of a loss of differentiation. A case in point is TV advertising time lengths. In the United States, 15-second advertisements had increased by 70 per cent in the five years through 2010, to the point where they accounted for 34 per cent of all ads in the United States. Mike Sheldon, CEO of Deutsch in Los Angeles, commented, "it becomes a very seductive thing to get your message out there at half the cost."[39] Mathematically this is correct, but a message is not a mathematical equation.

Hovis, a well-established brand of bread in the UK, went against this trend and produced an advertisement that was initially 122 seconds long and was then cut down to 90 and 10 second lengths. Already in just the time length there was a strong differentiator, with so much more space being given to the ad and thus making it stand out from the vast majority of other time lengths, irrespective of its actual message. But what it had to say was strong; it was an epic historical record of the brand over the years, with the theme "as good as it's always been". No doubt, in mathematical terms it would have been seen as indulgent and illogical – the media numbers would not stack up. Yet there is one set of numbers that is much more important than the media ones – the sales figures. These passed even the most rigorous mathematical scrutiny. In one year, sales increased by 14 per cent against a decline in the previous two years. Rough calculations of the net return arrived at a figure of £75.5 million, which represented a fivefold multiple on the marketing investment of £15 million.

It is reasonable to conclude that the success of this advertisement was not just due to the message itself but to the added impact it had by having such a long time length in a situation where the figures dictated shorter ones. A similar coup was effected by Barilla pasta in Italy in the 1980s, when the advertising industry was seduced by 15-second ads and Barilla produced a 90-second one. The result was an impact that transcended the cost of the campaign.

Upsetting the context

It is also important to remember the delicate balance which is sometimes the nature of context and how it can be upset in a way which negates attempts at differentiation. In the United States Kraft introduced DiGiorno Rising Crust Pizza, creating a high-quality tier in the frozen pizza category. The company anticipated that the new product would cannibalise Tombstone, a mid-tier Kraft pizza. But a study using long-term metrics showed that DiGiorno had a consequence that Kraft had not anticipated: the new product did not just steal sales from Tombstone but caused its price premium – and that of all mid-tier pizza brands – to drop sharply. It appeared that DiGiorno had made the mid-tier brands seem more ordinary to consumers. As a result, Tombstone was less able to withstand discounting from other pizzas like it. Ultimately, the introduction of DiGiorno was highly profitable for Kraft, but the company, unaware of the effect on Tombstone's price premium, may have overstated the profitability of the launch for its overall business.[40]

2 The intrinsic

The inner strength of differentiation

The English novelist Jeanette Winterson commented on how, at an early age, she "realised something important: whatever is on the outside can be taken away, only what is inside you is safe."[41] This is evident in the power of a firm or person's reputation, which relies completely on their perceived intrinsic merits. This recognition of the importance of the intrinsic is echoed on a wider scale in the insistence by vulnerable groups of people, such as the Jews and now the Palestinians, on education. It is something that can serve them wherever they are and can never be taken away from them – for it is inside them, not outside. This sums up the inner strength which is provided by what is intrinsic, rather than extrinsic.

The siren call of celebrity

A particular example of the latter in marketing is apparent in the cult of celebrity. In most cases the adoption of a celebrity appears to be the result of creative shortcomings and a failure to find an idea based on the intrinsic properties of the brand. There are examples where the celebrity can reflect the intrinsic aspects, such as the use of the celebrity chef Jamie Oliver in the UK by Sainsbury's, the supermarket chain, which was a great success. But these are rare. They might perform a trick on the consumer with a temporary sizzle, but this does not give the long-term underwriting that an intrinsic property can provide.

Marc Mathieu, Unilever's SVP marketing, argued that the use of famous faces must "be believable". However, celebrities who are completely in tune with the brand and reflect it are rare. Usually the approach is that of one-celebrity-fits-all, as in the use of the footballer Cristiano Ronaldo in advertising for Castrol engine oil – a brand which already had an enduring and powerful idea – that of "liquid engineering". Nespresso, Nestlé's coffee range, used the actor George Clooney in its international advertising. The normal explanation for such use of celebrities is that they help sales by linking the brand with certain values which the individual is deemed to embody. That the brand cannot be linked to its own values but has to rent those of someone else underlines the extrinsic nature of the exercise. Nespresso's chief executive, Richard Girardot, felt that Clooney was appropriate, as "he's a worldwide citizen, a democrat, a humanist". These are values which would appear rather too lofty for consumers to associate with coffee pods and espresso machines; to suggest that they should be aware of such a link can only leave them bemused.

It is instructive that very few of the IPA Effectiveness Awards – the most rigorous recognition of marketing success – are for campaigns with celebrities. Certainly the number awarded is completely disproportionate to the plethora of campaigns lazily (or is it desperately?) reaching for the cloak of celebrity. When Robert Polet arrived at Gucci as CEO, he scrapped any advertising with celebrities, stating that his desire was to make the brand, not the talent, the star. Subsequently Gucci did run a campaign featuring a celebrity, but one who was relevant – Guccio Gucci, its founder. The potential distraction of celebrity was well recognised by Steve Jobs when it was suggested that he provide the voiceover for an iMac commercial: "If we use my voice, when people find out they will say it's about me. It's not. It's about Apple."[42]

Polet's outlook was reflected by Jean-François van Boxmeer, Heineken's CEO. Heineken had featured Jennifer Aniston and Brad Pitt in different campaigns. "He was too central. It was a promotion for Brad Pitt, not Heineken," Boxmeer said. "You do that from time to time, but it is absolutely not central to our strategy." They now only follow this course sparingly.[43] Such comments highlight the danger of celebrities becoming like cuckoos in the brand nest.

An overall perspective on this issue was provided by the German magazine *Brigitte*, which conducted a survey in 2012 into the different rating between brands and personalities.[44] It was found that some brands, such as Nivea, Aldi and Dr Oetker, were seen as more likeable and credible than leading celebrities by a majority of German women. In addition, many women had negative things to say about some celebrities, even though they may have perceived them as being successful.

The price pit

But the most pervasive adoption of an extrinsic factor is price. This is a trap into which a brand can easily fall. Price can undermine the brand as, not being intrinsic to it, any move on price discounting can be answered by the competition, and often a price war can result which benefits neither party. A price advantage can be taken away while, by definition, something intrinsic to the brand cannot. There are exceptions to this, when price is not allowed to overrule intrinsic aspects as explained by Ingvar Kampred, the founder of IKEA: "they must be low prices with a meaning. We must not compromise either functionality or technical quality."[45] So low prices were not an end in themselves but had to be built on quality.

A particular area where differentiation is provided by the intrinsic properties of a brand is that of wine. The wines from individual vineyards have strong characteristics and are reinforced by the French concept of terroir, which glorifies the location of the vineyard in terms of its physical characteristics, such as the soil, climate and so on. In Burgundy a vineyard that is only a short distance from one producing the most expensive wine can only command an average price. An example of the difference these intrinsic properties can create is provided by the profits they can generate. In 2011 Cheval Blanc was reported to have made profits of €14 million on sales of €22 million, and Chateau Lafite Rothschild made €70.2 million on a turnover of €80.8 million.[46]

In fact wines have some of the most compelling elements for differentiation of almost any food or drink product. Not only is there the more physical aspect of terroir referred to previously, but there is also what might be called "emotional terroir", which is the unique aspect of the wine such as its history, those who make it and any unique anecdotes which, appealing to the emotions, have an even greater pull than just product details in terms of making clear differentiation. An example of this is Fleurie wine from Beaujolais, which is known as "the queen of Beaujolais". Yet this description is never used. Unfortunately those within the industry are blind to the broad palette for differentiation which wines provide. The ultimate result of this is that wine is one of the most heavily promoted categories in the UK grocery trade. Shoppers aren't naive; regular sales promotions encourage them to wait for the next sale rather than purchase a product at full price. The consumer has been educated to buy whatever is being promoted, which they have a tendency to do, to the exclusion of any intrinsic properties a wine might have which could differentiate it. The industry generally downgrades these points of differentiation and focuses on the extrinsic aspect of price, and thus moves a sector which has some of the firmest foundations for brands toward commoditisation.

A salutary tale was provided in the United States by Vlasic, which for fifty years was a beloved brand in America's kitchen cupboards. The brand departed from its intrinsic properties when it started discounting its pickles by offering them in gallon-size jars in the late 1990s. Walmart began selling the product for an unheard-of price of $2.99. This price was so low that Walmart soon made up 30 per cent of Vlasic's business. The super-cheap gallon jar cannibalised Vlasic's other channels and shrank its margins by

25 per cent. When Vlasic asked for pricing relief, Walmart responded by refusing an immediate price increase and reviewing its commitments to the brand. By 2001, Vlasic had filed for bankruptcy.

Walmart and other powerful retailers have undoubtedly weakened some brands, as has been the case with wine in the UK, but a number of consumer-product companies have done a better job than Vlasic in managing both their relationships with retailers and their brands. When Foot Locker cut Nike orders by about $200 million to protest the terms Nike had placed on prices and selection, Nike cut its allocation of shoes to Foot Locker by $400 million. Consumers, frustrated because they couldn't find the shoes they wanted, stopped shopping at Foot Locker. Sales at a competitor, Finish Line, increased. In the end, Foot Locker acceded to Nike's terms.

At the core of the differences in how Vlasic and Nike managed their brands is a crucial disparity in strategic perspective. By acceding to the focus on price demanded by Walmart, Vlasic eroded its intrinsic differences and indeed reduced advertising by 40 per cent between 1995 and 1998. Nike, on the other hand, maintained strong relationships with a variety of retailers and invested in brand equity, allocating $1.2 billion annually to its advertising budget.[47]

In terms of marketing, this was put into wider context in the US election campaign of 2016. The success of Donald Trump was a surprise to all, given the scepticism that greeted his entering the race. At the core of his achievement was an approach put forward by his campaign manager, Corey Lewandowski, of "let Trump be Trump". This involved allowing Trump to speak in his characteristically open and brash manner, an approach which put Lewandowski at odds with others within the campaign as well as donors and political allies. But the focus on Trump's intrinsic traits proved to be a winning strategy for obtaining the Republican nomination and ultimately the presidency. Being particular to him, they were unique and so gave him a marked differentiation from the other contenders who had a tendency to sink into political clichés, echoing each other and confirming the prejudice against the political establishment for which Trump was seen as a welcome antidote.

This same observation applies to a brand. If something is adopted which comes from the outside, then it is available for any competitor to take and so leaves the brand vulnerable, as this aspect can no longer be a point of differentiation. This is evident in the enthusiasm for "lifestyle" advertising where an off-the-peg approach is adopted without recognising that it is just as easy for a competitor to put on the same garment. In contrast, a bespoke suit is unique to the wearer, as it directly reflects him or her and so can be worn by no one else. Something from inside the brand, which is intrinsic, cannot be adopted by the competition. This is not to diminish the task of finding what will be the most compelling proposition for the consumer, but rather to clearly define the area of exploration, with its borders marked out by the brand itself.

A good example of how superficial a focus on the extrinsic aspects of a product can become is provided by a tale of the benighted Brussels sprout in the UK. Although it is a traditional part of the Christmas feast, its inclusion is often on sufferance. Each year there is a debate around how to help this humble legume. BBC radio called on no lesser an authority than the head of Interbrand, the international brand consultants. Her suggestion was the use of packaging. This is clearly an extrinsic feature, with no relevance to the intrinsic properties of the sprout. No account seemed to have been taken of the prosaic nature of the product, which is, after all, on a par with potatoes. Special packaging for these appeared to be an absurd suggestion.

Unfortunately the role of the experts such as the head of Interbrand has been elevated to a level approaching infallibility, so any viewpoint is seldom challenged. Even the Swedish chef in the Muppets showed greater strategic understanding when he threw a cabbage in the air and then blasted it with a blunderbuss. Down rained Brussels sprouts – positioning them as mini cabbages! At least this provided an intrinsic base for differentiation. French apple producers made great inroads into the UK market with a concept based on the properties of their apples. They simply talked of "Le Crunch". On reflection, this is also an intrinsic property of the sprout. So why could it not have been exploited?

In their bestselling book *Nudge*, Thaler and Sunstein summed up the basic concept:

> small and apparently insignificant details can have major impacts on people's behaviour. A good rule of thumb is to assume that "everything matters". Often, the power of these small details comes from focusing the attention of users in a particular direction.[48]

This was echoed by no lesser an expert than Sherlock Holmes many years earlier when he declared: "You know my method. It is founded on the observation of trifles."[49] The weight that apparently small details can have with a person over ones which appear more momentous was illustrated by cognitive neuroscientist Professor Sarah-Jayne Blakemore, quoting from an entry in the diary of a teenager on 20 July 1969:

> I went to the Arts Centre by myself in yellow chords and blouse. Ian was there, but didn't speak to me. Got rhyme put in my bag by someone who apparently has a crush on me. It's Nicholas, I think – ugh! Man landed on moon.[50]

The general observation on the power of apparently small details has as much validity in marketing as it does in most other spheres of human persuasion; in fact, it is an area where a nudge can be particularly potent. On the wider plain, this fits in with Wordsworth's description of creativity as "passive awareness". Those looking for differentiation need to be always mindful that it can come from the most unlikely quarters, which only serves to heighten the importance of seizing it as it flits by.

A sound piece of marketing advice was given by the Greek philosopher Epictetus in the first century: "know first who you are and then adorn yourself accordingly". Anything a brand does needs to be congruent with itself. Robin Wight, a prominent figure in UK advertising, looked at it from another perspective, two millennia later, when he coined the phrase "product interrogation", where you "interrogate the product until it confesses to its strengths". Such a forensic approach, combined with thought and insight, can provide differentiation for any brand, through patience and application. Often there is the complaint that no differentiation can be found. The only thing which this indicates is laziness and a lack of curiosity. If none exists, then the product has no right to be a brand.

The important of curiosity is paramount, but it must be conducted within parameters of relevance to the brand and its intrinsic qualities. Many preen themselves on "thinking outside the box". But if this strays from the brand then, however dazzling the thought, it can have little practical relevance as, at the end of the day, it needs to get back inside the box. As David Robertson noted when writing about LEGO and their impressive turnaround from near bankruptcy in the early 2000s, "they give their development teams wide latitude to create, so long as they innovate 'inside the box.'"[51] He explained further that "when LEGO succeeds . . . it innovates from the inside out. That is, the development team starts with its core capabilities." In other words, their start-point is always what is intrinsic to the brand and the company.

A good example of the garden path up which extrinsic solutions can lead is provided by the launch of Windows Vista. Here there appeared to be no clarity as to how the brand was different, so the advertising fell back on the vacuous word "wow". If there had been a clear difference, then it could have been articulated to the consumer. A constructive start-off point would have been to find out which areas of the previous Windows software consumers thought might be improved and then incorporate these improvements in the Vista software, giving a reason for its introduction as opposed to presenting it as flavour of the month.

Without any explanation as to what "wow" was about, the advertising appeared to have little meaning other than amazement at something about which no one had a clue. It became an article of faith. There was no point of differentiation for the consumer to latch onto and to feel that it was a real advance over previous software. This advertising indicated that any difference had eluded even Microsoft itself. Ironically, it was regarded as one of Microsoft's most unsuccessful software packages

An example of the interrogation referred to by Wight is a small UK confectionery brand called Rowntree's Fruit Pastilles. A strategy was developed in 1976 for this brand, after examining and tasting the product. This resulted in the simple observation that once in the mouth, it was difficult to resist chewing. This insight spawned the Rowntree's Fruit Pastilles Chewing Challenge advertising campaign, which involved betting different celebrities that they couldn't resist chewing. It continues today, forty years later. This differentiation of Fruit Pastilles had focused on something intrinsic, which could not be taken away and so was sustainable over time.

Insights into the intrinsic

Insight is defined as seeing what others don't, and this can happen with an intrinsic property of a brand which nobody has previously recognised as giving a point of differentiation. This was the case with Motrin in Canada, where the simple observation was that three is better than two. Motrin is an analgesic and was making no progress against Advil, the market leader, as there was neither product difference nor innovation available. The basis for the insight was research which indicated that each person sees their pain as unique and wants to choose pain relief based on their own personal assessment as to the level of their pain.

The exploitation of this through the intrinsic properties of Motrin was based on the fact that Advil came in only two sizes: Regular 200 mg and Extra 400 mg. Motrin, in contrast, offered three: Regular 200 mg, Extra 300 mg and Super Strength 400 mg. This seemingly prosaic and mundane difference, which had always been there, combined with the insight from the research allowed Motrin to promise that "whatever the level of pain, Motrin has your relief". This exploitation of such a simple point of differentiation resulted in an increase of 40 per cent in Motrin's share in just one year.[52]

In the UK, Saab simply looked at itself and came up with a point of differentiation which had also always been there but, as with Motrin, no one had bothered with. The company had been performing badly in the UK, with the price of their cars being unable to even keep up with the increases in the retail price index as large discounts had to be offered to achieve sales – not the best approach for what was supposed to be a premium brand. The intrinsic fact which was seized upon was that Saab had been involved in the arms industry for many years, making several generations of fighter jets for the Swedish air force. Research indicated that this involvement was unique and highly motivating – the analogy of a Saab driver with a fighter pilot represented a direct hit on the emotions. This was used in the advertising, with an emotive commercial of a Saab car and fighter jet, enshrined in a simple description of Saab as "the aircraft manufacturer". Within three years sales took off. They increased by 71 per cent and profits by 331 per cent.[53]

An even more solid example of the power of the intrinsic and also how easily solid bases can be sacrificed is provided by BMW. They managed to achieve a successful image through building around the proposition of "the ultimate driving machine". Much comment on this campaign focused on the strength of the advertising line. This does not pay proper recognition to the fact that this would have been much less compelling, had it not been firmly rooted in facts about the car – the line would have hovered above the brand with little direct connection.

To provide this substance, BMW ran a campaign based on individual aspects of the car. This might be called a pixel approach, whereby an overall picture is established by describing each individual dot. Such a strategy has been used successfully by other brands, most notably Tesco in the UK, where each "pixel" of detail regarding what they offered contributed to building a picture for the brand to support the line, "every little helps". Interestingly Tesco deviated from this approach for many years by simply talking about the extrinsic aspect of price as the basis for this line. It lost share. Only when it brought back stories about intrinsic aspects of Tesco, so giving the line some real meaning, did its share begin to recover.

Not only was the BMW advertising referred to highly successful in terms of advancing their share; the power of the idea paid in financial effectiveness. In 2008 BMW was top in terms of rate of return on advertising spending per car in the UK. The amount spent between 1 January and 31 August 2008 worked out at only £22 for each new car registered, less than 10 per cent of the national average of £233 per vehicle. The next most successful manufacturer was Ford at £114. That other paragon of German success – Volkswagen – spent £155 per car.[54]

Unfortunately, to the outsider, it then appeared that BMW's campaign regressed to a state for which the term "hovering" might be used. In contrast to the previous solid rooting in the product, it adopted a positioning around the nebulous and generic property of "joy" to support the claim of the ultimate driving machine which was, in turn, based on woolly generic properties such as "balance" and "control", which had no particular foundation in BMW. To the uninformed, this seems as vacuous as the frequent repetition of people saying "wow", which Microsoft used for the launch of its Vista software.

Turning an intrinsic negative into a positive

Often a brand can feel it has been dealt a bad hand when there are characteristics which are regarded as negatives and every effort is made to either remove them or skirt around them. One of the most prominent is Marmite, a yeast extract spread in the UK. This has a very distinctive taste which many hate and others love. Rather than denying this reality, Marmite embraced it and came up with the line "You either love it or hate it". It has not only made the yeast spread memorable, but has also helped the name become part of the English language. "Marmite" is now often used to describe events or people which are polarising.

Another example is Orangina, the French carbonated orange-based drink. The particular cross which this brand apparently had to bear was that the manufacturing process resulted in there being a residue of pulp at the bottom of the bottle. For long this was regarded as a troubling negative until it was decided to accept this supposed handicap and make it into a differentiator, with the line "Shake the bottle, wake the drink".

Finally there is Guinness, with its supposed albatross of the need to pour the drink very slowly when serving: it has been calculated that it takes 119.5 seconds to pour and serve a perfect pint of Guinness. Many attempts were made to get rid of this inconvenience, sometimes utilizing tricks of technology. But rather than these forlorn manoeuvres, the most enduring result was the line "Good things come to those who wait", variously interpreted over many advertising campaigns and a keystone of Guinness's position and success. This tapped in to an observation from Winnie the Pooh that the moment just before eating the honey is better than when you are eating it. Anticipation is a powerful emotion.

The Guinness example is also a good illustration of the power of ritual, which can itself become distinctive. It can become a small story in itself which, in turn, helps differentiate the product. The story aspect was well explained by Jonathan Ive, the chief designer of Apple, when commenting on the importance of the packaging he developed: "I love the process of unpacking something. You design a ritual of unpacking to feel the product feels special. Packaging can be theatre, it can create a story."[55] This was echoed by the reality contest star, Susan Boyle, when she commented on receiving a present bought at Tiffany's: "the ritual of opening the gift is always better than the gift."[56] Indeed there is a word in German, "Wohlverpackungsfreude", which means the "uncomplicated delight of a well-wrapped parcel". Such was the importance which Apple gave to packaging that many of the designs were patented. Indeed the cost of each computer case was over $60, three times that of a regular one. Such an approach contributed to a particularly scathing comment on Apple's differentiation from Joseph Graziano, a former CFO of the company, who felt that

> Apple's problem is it still believes the way to grow is serving caviar in a world that seems pretty content with cheese and crackers.[57]

History has proved otherwise. One particular point of difference I've incorporated in the design was a recessed handle for, as I've explained, people weren't comfortable with technology . . . If you're scared of something, then you won't touch it. So I thought, if there's a handle on it, it makes a relationship possible, it's intuitive.

3 Telling a unique story

Often a brand can be differentiated by the simplest way in which people distinguish themselves – by telling a story about itself. The importance of this process was highlighted by Gavin Fairburn of Leeds University, who noted, "storytelling is central to most of human life. It is also the most startlingly simple and direct way I know of encouraging the development of empathy". Julian Baggini summed it up by observing that "humans make sense of their world by telling stories."[58] In his book, *Mindwise*, Nicholas Epley gave more flesh to this when he stated that

> you define yourself not by the attributes that make you the same as everyone else – has two arms, two legs, breathes air – but rather by the attributes which make you different from everyone else – spent time in the Peace Corps, works as a physicist, loves to go fishing, and so on.[59]

This further illustrates the importance of focusing on the intrinsic because, in doing so, any personal story will be, by definition, unique. Even scientists, Daniel Kahneman observed, are far more likely to persuade people by telling them stories than by giving them facts.[60] Indeed he stated that; "no-one ever made a decision because of a number. They need a story."[61] On the business front, Lucy Kellaway observed that "experts everywhere are waking up to the something that any child could tell them: that a story is easier to listen to and much easier to remember than a dry set of facts and propositions."[62]

Above all, stories are helpful in providing the differentiation through intrinsic aspects, which facilitates the establishment of relationships that are fundamental in terms of connecting to a brand just as to a person. The Israeli philosopher Martin Buber categorised all relationships as being either I-It (with objects) or I-Thou (with people). As a relationship moves along this spectrum and gets closer to I-Thou, it reaches a point of empathy.

The essence of a brand is to move along this axis, from the inanimate functional state of I-It toward the organic, empathetic and emotional state of I-Thou. Stories can be particularly effective in achieving this, in line with Fairburn's comment that storytelling was the most effective way he knew of developing empathy.

Consequently, the use of stories in marketing is simply tapping into a fundamental human trait – always a good foundation for any communication. Although they can be a strong competitive weapon, it is worth pointing out that seldom do stories need to have an overt competitive edge. Usually all the story has to do is establish how the brand is different from its competitors, thanks to the uniqueness of its story, and leave the rest to the consumer. It is a subtle form of persuasion, as there is no overt selling message in the story, yet it establishes a competitive advantage through the possession of a simple narrative. Given that this is a fundamental human trait, it has unsurprisingly been commented on over the years, starting with Aristotle, and was echoed more recently by the neurologist Joseph Le Doux when he pointed out that "persuasion always works better when the persuadee is not aware that he or she is being persuaded."[63]

An example of how simple stories have worked has been the success of Jack Daniel's,[64] which has built itself into the sixth-biggest drinks brand in the world and the single biggest whiskey brand by differentiating itself through a series of individual stories firmly rooted in its hometown of Lynchburg and in the people who make it. The style of these was summed up by their being referred to as "postcards". Such an approach is a good illustration of the "emotional terroir" of a brand referred to in the discussion about wines, where the positioning springs directly from the intrinsic nature of the brand's context and the firm emotional base this provides. Unlike the more short-sighted obsessions of the wine industry, there is seldom any mention of taste nor of the product. These are aspects the consumer can find out for themselves when they consume it. In order to be considered an enduring story, it needs to be something which they cannot directly discover yet can become part of their personal perception of the brand. As the creative director said, "We're not selling a bottle of booze. We're selling a place." The campaign has lasted for more than sixty years. It is instructive that when the brand went into overseas markets, the local agencies often wanted to use campaigns based on the hackneyed default for alcohol advertising of lifestyle – an extrinsic property. Campaigns based on this approach were tested against "postcards." The latter always won.

Ted Simmons, the copywriter, described his approach to writing Jack Daniel's ads as "wanderin' around." He would sit on the bench in front of The Iron Kettle restaurant, wander next door to the farmers' co-op and try to hear what the farmers were talking about, wander into the bank, and then up to the hardware store to sit with Clayton Tosh by the pot-bellied stove. Then he'd visit Tolley's Wishy Washy Laundromat, named after one of the first head distillers at Jack Daniel's. Or drink lemonade at the White Rabbit Saloon, which no longer served alcohol since Moore County is bone-dry – an ironic fact celebrated in one commercial. After wandering, he would go back to the original office of the founders Jack Daniel and his successor Lem Motlow, and try to imagine what they might say about what was happening in Jack Daniel's Hollow. Obviously such wandering did not serve any rational or overtly competitive argument, but simply helped gather more twigs to stoke the emotional fire.

The campaign started in 1954. One of only two ad men to openly praise the campaign at the time was advertising giant David Ogilvy, who wrote to the distillery saying: "If there is a better campaign in your industry, I have never seen it. Indeed, I would rank it among the half dozen best campaigns in the history of advertising." Through this advertising, Jack Daniels built up a unique folksy and intimate picture with the evocative emotional values of small-town USA. Perversely, the campaign has received no advertising awards, but its success in terms of a more important criterion is clear as the brand grew from 100,000 cases in 1955 to over twelve million cases today (for its core Black Label variety) and world leadership. The impression-ability of the advertising industry is well illustrated by this omission from its accolades and its tendency to hail cinematic bombast, as was evident in the Apple 1984 and Guinness White Horses ads mentioned later. Neither of these could lay claim to anything approaching the business miracle performed by the Jack Daniel's campaign.

In marked contrast to this carefully considered and curated campaign is the approach of many in the wine industry who take a rather supercilious and ignorant approach to marketing. This was best illustrated by a wine critic in *The Observer* Sunday paper. He wrote about how with a wine, "it's the one with the more straightforward package that gets my cash every time – the one that suggests the producer has spent their time and money on the contents rather than dreaming up an unnecessary 'brand story'". This showed a basic ignorance of the fact that a story needs only a little curiosity and that it certainly does not need "dreaming up"; if it is intrinsic to the brand – the only sort of story worth telling – then it is already there. Also it is puzzling why something which can have such potency in selling a brand should be deemed "unnecessary". Ironically, this apparent disdain was immediately contradicted the next week when he focused his review of a wine from Greece on the fact that it was from a small producer who made it as a sideline from her main profession as a doctor. He talked about it being an example of "little-guy revenge *stories*". Such blinkered prejudice in the face of anything which might smack of marketing, even though the idea of a story is in fact embraced, gives some indication as to how the wine industry has, through combining neglect and ignorance of marketing, fostered a tendency to commoditisation and so become such a prey to the siren call of price promotions. Such behaviour is well characterised by the aphorism "volume is vanity, profit is sanity", as short-term volume gain sacrifices long-term profitability.

Given the need for a brand to develop an emotional link with the consumer, focusing on its own story can create a compelling bond. Labatt's Alexander Keith's India Pale Ale had been brewed in Halifax, Nova Scotia, since 1820 and was the number one beer in eastern Canada. There had been a change in the market which gave an opportunity for Alexander Keith's to expand beyond its traditional territory. Mainstream beers were beginning to be seen as generic and consumers were attracted by beers that came from somewhere different or had a distinctive story. The market began to fragment due to the growing popularity of microbreweries, imports and speciality beers.

The brand had developed primarily as a draft beer, and as a result, the main consumer was in his late twenties and thirties, a group which consumed less than younger men. Consequently, the brewery decided to speak to slightly younger drinkers – aged twenty-five to thirty – who appreciated a more sophisticated beer. In talking to them, Labatt's homed in on the fact that speciality beer drinkers needed to feel validated by their choice of beer. These consumers put more thought into selecting a beer and the brand became a badge they were proud to display.

The heritage of Alexander Keith's had all the elements to meet this requirement; it was just a question of how these attributes would be presented. They were distilled into a simple proposition: "Alexander Keith's is the pride of Nova Scotia. A pride worthy of respect." This built on stories of the brand's brewing heritage, a rich history and a legend centred on the brewmaster, Alexander Keith. It was further developed into the idea that there was a certain etiquette required in drinking the beer, playing to the attitudes that had been identified in the target group – much like Guinness had for years capitalised on its slow pouring. A year and a half later, the brand's share had grown by 33 per cent in Ontario and the west of Canada, and it had become the number one speciality beer in Canada.[65]

Stories adding value

The practical importance of stories was examined in an experiment called Significant Objects.[66] This was to test the hypothesis that "narrative transforms the insignificant into the significant". Put differently, the exercise was to determine whether an object with little worth could command a higher price by giving it a story. This follows the observation by Ariely in *Predictably Irrational* that "marketing is all about providing information that will heighten someone's anticipated and real pleasure".[67]

The project's originators – *New York Times* columnist Rob Walker and author Josh Glenn – bought one hundred garage sale items for no more than a few dollars each, and then had volunteer writers produce fictional stories about them. They supposed that this would increase the perceived value of the items. And they were right. At the garage sale they paid a total of $128.74, but when combined with stories the same goods went for a total of $3,612.51 on eBay. In a way they were no longer just objects but repositories of stories, which increased the ease with which the purchaser could relate to them and so gave them greater value. A similar exercise was carried out by an advertising agency in Melbourne. They bought a BMX bike on eBay for $27.50 and, by constructing a whacky narrative around it, were able to sell it for $134.50, a nearly 500 per cent increase in its perceived worth.[68]

Another example of stories giving a substantial increase in value was provided by the LEGO Architecture line. This was initiated by Adam Reed Tucker, a Chicago architect who, on his own initiative, started building skyscrapers made with LEGOs. The first example he showed LEGO was a model of the Sears (now Willis) Tower in Chicago. In addition to instructions, the booklet that came with the bricks had a brief profile of the architect, the origin of the design and the architectural features. Tucker said, "I wanted to tell a story, not just sell a box of bricks."[69]

The resulting range of LEGO Architecture took the bricks into many new areas. Also the company felt that the bricks could be sold at a substantial premium over other LEGO sets. This was despite the fact that LEGO bricks already retailed at twice the price of equivalent ones. Any manufacturer could make identical bricks, as the last patent had expired in 1989. This is an example of how well a brand can underwrite a price differential. But the LEGO Architecture sets built even further on this, with their clear differentiation through the new architectural context of the bricks underwritten by the stories. A box of seventy normal LEGO bricks sold for $7.99, whereas an Architecture box containing the same number of the same standard bricks sold at $19.99. Since the line's launch in 2008 the sales increased by 900 per cent in 2009, 350 per cent in 2010 and 200 per cent in 2011. Although the exact financial details were kept confidential, the range was, unsurprisingly, described by a senior LEGO executive as "very, very profitable".

On a much more detailed level are the short stories that Farrow and Ball,[70] a UK producer of premium paint and wallpaper, uses to give a greater depth to the colours they sell. They invented a completely new range of names for their colours, such as "Smoked Trout", "Mizzle" and "Nancy's Blushes", which became talking points in their own right. But none of the names were left as empty words as each was given a short story. The colour called Calke Green is described as "a cleaned version of a colour originally found in the Breakfast Room at Calke Abbey". On the website each colour has a short thirty-two second video presented by an International Colour Consultant, Colour Consultancy Manager or Head of Creative, who explain the background and the best way to use each particular paint.

The difference in the quality of the paint is firmly underwritten by this approach. The result of this establishment and recounting of intrinsic qualities helps Farrow and Ball charge £74.50 for a five litre can of "Wimborne White", whereas Dulux, the mainstream paint brand, charges £27.50 for five litres of their "Timeless Silk Emulsion". In addition, Farrow and Ball's paint is a little more difficult to apply and so painters will charge extra for using it. All this amounts to a substantial premium for which the product, the unique vocabulary and the stories produce clear differentiation. The strength of Farrow and Ball's position is both illustrated and underwritten by the fact that they give no discounts on their prices, nor do they allow any retailers to do so.

A very specific example of the power of a story is provided by the Flexo lamp and its marketing in the UK. This is a small aluminium table lamp from Spain, much beloved of students there for the simple fact that it is cheap. In its home country it is not even sold in lighting shops, but in dusty boxes at the back of hardware stores. Consequently, the dominating characteristic of this lamp was the extrinsic one – its price. This overshadowed appreciation of the lamp for any of its intrinsic merits.

It had an attractive design and it was felt that, rather than being sold purely on price, it could be sold as an accessible object of design – a lamp equivalent of the Zippo lighter. In addition, there were few actual brands in the lamp market; rather there were manufacturers' and catalogue names. Consequently, Flexo could establish its position in the new market of the UK by being a brand. In order to support this, a distinctive logo was developed and a story was unearthed which was featured on the lamp and shelf cards. The simple wording was "The Flexo is an integral part of Spanish life, having been in continuous production since 1925. Although the designer is unknown, the Flexo is a design classic, a version being in the Design Museum in London."

This provided a solid springboard to success, as the lamp received press coverage in the UK of more than thirty million readers. It sold well in many of the principal design stores and branched out into chains, such as Habitat. The perceptions of it were radically different from those in its homeland, with the *Sunday Times* describing it as "a masterpiece of modern design". The approach used for the Flexo was simple but effective, built around a short meaningful story that was intrinsic to the brand. It was this unique story which differentiated the lamp from others on the market, none of which told the consumers any stories or even presented themselves as brands, and transformed it from a cheap table lamp in Spain to an accessible design object in the UK, as its retail price was only £25.00

Unfortunately all this work was undone by marketing myopia when the Spanish manufacturer chose to sell direct to a British home furnishing store which was the largest retailer of the lamp. Both were blinded by the idea of selling it cheap and were unable to use the brand name, which was registered, or the story. Consequently they sold it under the empty catalogue name of "Felix" at a low price, without any other redeeming features. Such blinkered short-sightedness resulted in the end of the lamp in the UK after a few brief years, although it occasionally surfaces in films where it is used as part of the set of an interior portraying a strong design theme, such as the 2014 British film *Exhibition*. At least its intrinsic values are sometimes recognised, albeit fleetingly.

"We could double Bowmore's volume by halving the price, but we want to build long-term value" – these were the words of the marketing director of Bowmore, a producer of malt whisky. They sum up a familiar dilemma when tackling a market, and show a healthy awareness of the bottom line rather than being seduced by the siren call of volume and share, which have enticed so many marketing plans and brands onto the rocks.

Bottled whisky accounted for 44 per cent of Bowmore's volume and 78 per cent of its value. This was because the majority of its product was sold in bulk as a commodity. At the time, supermarkets were beginning to wield more power in this sector (as they accounted for 64 per cent of sales) and were encouraging whisky brands to discount. The two main players in the malt whisky market – Glenfiddich and Glenmorangie – were acceding to these demands and diverting money from above the line to fund heavier discounting.

By contrast Bowmore took the opposite course and used advertising as leverage to help dissuade retailers from demanding discounts. Taking such a risk needed a strong point of differentiation which, through assiduous research, they were able to winkle out of the product. As a programme on food on BBC radio stated, "a truly great whisky should give a sense of place".[71] Bowmore reflected this, as it is a malt from the island of Islay and is characterised by a peaty/smoky taste which gives it a more complex character and a more challenging taste than its two main competitors: Glenfiddich and Glenmorangie. These distinctive traits fuelled the proposition "surrender to the adventure" and to an expression of the Bowmore legend, based on folk tales from Islay which helped underwrite its sense of place.

In one year the average retail price of Bowmore went up 3 per cent. In contrast, for the market as a whole there was an average price decrease of 2 per cent. Bowmore became the fastest growing malt in the top 10 brands, with a volume increase of 36 per cent and an increase in value of 33 per cent. It was not able to avoid discounting completely, but while the average for the market was £5.00–6.00 per bottle, Bowmore managed to limit it to an average of just £3.50 – a valuable object lesson to those in the wine industry and a stark contrast to their surrender to commoditisation through promotions.[72]

Such awareness by Bowmore of the intrinsic differentiation that could be achieved through heritage also came to the aid of one of its main competitors, Glenmorangie. In looking at the name of the brand, they discovered that in Gaelic it meant "The Glen of Tranquillity". Although tranquillity was recognised as a generic property for whisky, Glenmorangie laid claim to it with its connotations of relaxation and quiet reflection, combined with the functional benefit of purity.

In the first year sales increased by 18 per cent in volume and 13 per cent in value, while in the most dynamic sector, the multiples, volume increased by 27 per cent. However, these increases were not at the expense of the bottom line, as the second year of this new positioning saw Glenmorangie achieve an increase in its average price premium over the sector of 56 per cent, which was largely due to an increase in the sales of its more expensive malts.[73]

Believability of a story

As to the believability of a story, its base can often be deceptively simple. Daniel Kahneman commented that

> the confidence that people experience is determined by the coherence of the story they manage to construct from the available information. It is the consistency of the information that matters for a good story, not its completeness. Indeed you will often find that knowing little makes it easier to fit everything you know into a coherent pattern . . . Much of the time the coherent story we put together is close enough to reality to support reasonable action.

The effect on the recipient is well articulated by Topolinski: "processing fluency increases both the positive effect and the judged truth".[74]

The effect of coherence for children was highlighted by Maryanne Wolf, who noted that "the more coherent the story is to the child, the more easily it is held in memory".[75] A story can be simple so long as it is coherent, and this latter quality can underwrite the perceptions the consumer forms regarding a brand. This observation was echoed by Robert McKee, a well-known writer on stories, who commented that "given the choice between trivial material brilliantly told versus profound material badly told, an audience will always choose the trivial told brilliantly".[76] He went on to say, "you might have the insight of the Buddha, but if you cannot tell a story, your ideas turn dry as chalk."[77]

One other significant piece of advice from Ann Booth-Clibborn, a consultant on the importance of stories for business, was always to tell one's own story and not to take it from someone else, as people will know when it is not authentic. This was echoed by Simon Beaufoy, the screenwriter for the multiple Oscar-winning film *Slumdog Millionaire*, who observed that "authenticity is the most important word for me in screenwriting. You can smell it a mile off, and you can smell the absence of it a mile off."[78] If the consumer can smell a rat in a film, they are just as likely to detect it in the way a brand presents itself.

4 It's not reality that needs to be different, but perceptions

In terms of differentiation there is often a mistaken belief that, if there is a difference in reality, then all that needs to be done is to point this out to the consumer and they will climb on board. This is lazy and naive. What matters to the consumer is not the objective reality but how it relates to themselves in terms of their beliefs. It is not a question of what it is but what they think it is. As Daniel Kahneman observed, "it's quite disturbing when you realise people consider facts irrelevant".[79] This was particularly noticeable in the surprising successes of Donald Trump's presidential election campaign. In response to many of his fanciful claims at their debates, Hillary Clinton frequently referred the audience with assurance to her "fact-checker". This showed her complete failure to grasp Kahneman's point. Her's was a perfectly logical and rational response but irrelevant in the context, as most of her audience didn't give a damn. Many in marketing think that the rational approach of presenting the facts is all that is required to persuade. If Trump was useful for one thing, it was in underlining the fallacy of this belief.

One of the most potent concepts in marketing, that of a brand, has come to be referred to as if it is a real thing when it is merely thoughts, being the sum of perceptions the consumer has of a particular product. Consumers' behaviour in relation to a product is based on their thoughts, which are gathered together in the concept of a brand – much like a bundle of reeds. Perception is the only currency which has any value. As Donald Norman, director of The Design Lab at University of California, San Diego, and author of *The Design of Everyday Things*, observed, "the causal relationship does not have to exist, the person simply has to think it's there – perception".[80]

The real force of perceptions is shown by the reaction in the United States to hurricanes. Researchers at the University of Illinois[81] found that hurricanes given female names tended to have more deadly results than ones with male names, because people's perceptions were that they would be less dangerous. The researchers at the university looked at six decades of death rates from US hurricanes and found that those with female names were more deadly because people perceived them as less threatening and therefore took fewer precautions to protect themselves.

A hurricane's name is unrelated to how fierce it will be, as male and female names are assigned alternately. The report suggested that changing a severe hurricane's name from Charley to Eloise could triple its death rate. "In judging the intensity of a storm, people appear to be applying their beliefs about how men and women behave", said study co-author Sharon Shavitt, a professor of marketing at the University of Illinois at Urbana-Champaign. "This makes a female-named hurricane, especially one with a very feminine name such as Belle or Cindy, seem gentler and less violent." In the second part of their study, which was published in the *Proceedings of the National Academy of Sciences*, the researchers asked participants about fake hurricanes with names like Hurricane Alexandra or Hurricane Alexander. Again, the participants rated the storms with female names as being less risky.

Another trick of perception was found in the more refined and elevated world of wine. In France, Frederic Brochet, a wine researcher, served fifty-seven French wine experts with two identical mid-range Bordeaux wines, one in an expensive Grand Cru bottle the other in a cheap Vin de Table bottle. The wine in the expensive bottle was preferred by a large majority. They used positive terms such as "excellent", "complex", "good" and "long" more than twice as often when describing this wine than when they talked about the wine in the cheap wine bottle. For the latter they used negative terms such as "unbalanced", "short", "flat" and "simple" more than twice as often. Yet it was exactly the same wine.[82] It is particularly refreshing to learn that even experts are subject to the same influences as ourselves, but then, as Kahneman and Tversky observed, we are all humans. It is always best to keep this in mind in order to keep our feet firmly on the ground, which is the best place for making any decisions.

The actual difference between perceptions and reality in marketing has been clearly established in real terms by the amount of time it takes for one to catch up with the other. This was observed by Mitra and Golder,[83] who conducted research into twenty-one products in forty-six categories over twelve years and found that the time for perceptions to adjust and accurately reflect the true quality of a product – the reality – was an average of 5.7 years. For some products, such as toothpaste, it was shorter; for others, like tyres, it was longer.

Interestingly this works both ways: when a brand elicits positive perceptions and the reality is falling short, it takes time for this to work through to how people regard it; just as when it has a negative image which it has in fact overcome in reality, it still takes a while for people's perceptions to fully reflect this. This was well illustrated in the car industry. The quality of Mercedes declined in the early 2000s, and it was marked down on industry surveys such as that of J.D. Power. But such was the strength of perceptions around it that they were able to put the reality right before the shortcomings worked through to how consumers thought of the brand. By contrast, Skoda in the UK had all the negative baggage of being a car which had been made in the former communist Czechoslovakia, where quality did not appear to be of paramount importance. This perception followed the brand even when it had been taken over by Volkswagen and had raised its game substantially. The advertising acknowledged the negatives full on by showing what appeared to be a very appealing car and ending with the line "It's a Skoda. Honest."

In terms of perceptions, it is not just the particular brand itself which can be enhanced by differentiation, but also associate brands. One of the best examples of this was the development of the Apple iPod. From the start, the idea was that the iPod would drive sales of the iMac as well as itself. Money was taken from the budget of the iMac to support the iPod in order to lend lustre and youthfulness to the iMac. As Steve Jobs put it, "I moved $75 million of advertising money to the iPod, even though the category didn't justify one hundredth of that. That meant we completely dominate the market for music players. We outspent everybody by a factor of about 100."[84] The iPod would position Apple as representing innovation and youth. Initially there had been some scepticism, particularly around the $399 price tag, the joke being that the name stood for "idiots price our devices". But this didn't stop it from being a big hit. As Jobs's biographer, Walter Isaacson, wrote, "when you took an iPod out of the box, it was so beautiful that it seemed to glow, and it made all other music players look as though they had been designed and manufactured in Uzbekistan."[85] It was launched in October 2001, and by 2005, twenty million were sold, four times the number of the year before. The brand by then accounted for 45 per cent of the company's revenue.

But even in terms of product, Jobs realised that a change had to be meaningful in terms of the differentiation that consumers perceived. The tablet was a product which Microsoft had been developing. A colleague of Jobs was friendly with the person at Microsoft who was involved in developing this new product and, on several occasions, invited Jobs to come over with him for dinner with this friend. This individual would brag about the tablet, much to the annoyance of Bill Gates, who came to one of the dinners. This proved too much for Jobs, who stated that "this dinner was like the tenth time he talked to me about it and I was so sick of it that I came home and said 'fuck this, let's show what a tablet can really be.'"[86] He felt he could make something different and better. In particular he had a profound antipathy to the use of a stylus, which the Microsoft tablet used. History indicates how it might have been better if the Microsoft employee had refrained from bragging.

There is also the fact that perceptions can arise because of the "cognitive miser" aspect of people referred to earlier. They can't be bothered to undergo the onerous task of thinking and would far rather plumb for what seems attractive, appealing to what Daniel Kahneman described as System 1 thinking. In his distinction of thinking between System 1 and System 2, the former "operates automatically and quickly with little or no effort and no sense of voluntary control".[87] By contrast, System 2 is more deliberative and is where reasoning takes place. Yet Kahneman regards it as subservient to System 1, as he writes, "I describe System 1 as effortlessly originating impressions and feelings that are the main sources of the explicit beliefs and deliberate choices of System 2."[88]

A good example of this is the sub-prime mortgages which contributed to the financial crisis of 2008. Most went along with them, as they had AAA ratings and so, as far as they were concerned, this status removed any need to check. It was only those who did bother to unbundle the sub-prime mortgages, as revealed in the book and film *The Big Short*, who discovered that their core was empty. A bundle of sticks is difficult to break, but it will soon snap if most of the reeds are rotten.

The unwillingness of people to work things out for themselves and to default to System 1 thinking is particularly evident in their aversion to any analysis with regard to financial matters. There was a time in the United States when reductions in the price of cars were replaced by rebates; one of $300 on the price of a car proved more alluring than a simple price reduction. But, given all the manufacturers were adopting this approach and its novelty had palled, the rebates began to lose their pull. They certainly provided no differentiation.

In reaction to this, General Motors looked at the going rate for a car loan. This was at 10 per cent or more. They offered either a rebate or a discounted loan at just 2.9 per cent. The reaction was almost hysterical, with news reports of consumers sprawled on the bonnets of cars at a dealership, claiming a particular car before anyone else could buy it.[89] But, as with *The Big Short*, a reporter had done the math and discovered that the value of the low interest loan was less than the value of the rebate. The perception arrived at by the use of System 1 thinking and laziness resulted in the triumph of perceptions over reality and a differentiator that was not real but perceived as such even more effective.

Avoid marketing what consumers can see/experience for themselves

Often the brand has achieved a real difference in product terms, which is clearly noticeable by the consumer. In terms of marketing this, differentiation has already done its job, and there is little point in repeatedly telling the consumer what they already know and can see in front of them. Yet often, particularly in areas such as taste, marketing tries to focus on areas where consumers can directly decide from their own experience. The bottom line is that the consumer either likes the taste of something or not; to keep repeating messages about taste is not sustainable. As in the example of Marmite quoted earlier, it is better to just accept the subjective opinion of the individual and move on from there.

There is only one occasion when the communication of physically noticeable differences is helpful – the first time the consumer considers the brand, as this might attract their choice. However once the product has been tried, then the consumer has made up their mind on the most important differentiator of all – whether they like it. Furthermore, any attempt at differentiation through what consumers can notice by themselves is redundant. What is required is a far more sustaining message which they cannot directly experience, an intangible one which is based on perceptions.

A striking example of this is the way wines are sold on their taste, with florid descriptions announcing their characteristics on the shelf cards and the bottle's label, which appear to have little relation to how the consumer actually rates a wine. There is no doubt that wine critics strenuously look for ways to articulate their experience of a wine, but this, in effect, is a search for fool's gold. The consumer would hardly ever use such language and is usually unlikely to detect the particular comparisons of taste which are presented, much as they might try. If they don't, there is always the chance that the customer might feel demeaned – never a good idea if one wants to build empathy for one's brand. Taste is a highly subjective area, and the repeated purchase of a wine relies on this. Even if the consumer was able to decipher these descriptions, they only have any real validity if they persuade them to buy for the first time. Once bought, then, if liked, there is the possibility of future purchase. But if the reception is negative, no amount of descriptive prose will make any difference to the decision not to buy. It is far more sustaining to focus on the intangibles which are the basis of perceptions – hence the power of stories, which has already been noted, as this is not something the consumer can confirm or invalidate subjectively, but is one of the layers of perception that are constructed on the core of reality which go to make up a brand. Stories are detached from the personal experience of the product by the consumer, which should have already been separately addressed when it was developed rather than being a part of the marketing of the brand.

One brand which transcended the blinkered focus on taste and product characteristics was Stella Artois in the UK. In its home country of Belgium, its position was that of a swilling lager, the lowest of the low. In addition to this negative baggage there was the reality that, in blind taste tests in the UK, Stella had a poor rating as it was felt to have a slightly bitter taste. But this setback was transcended through perceptions. The price was raised to make it into a premium lager, and then they had the audacity to sell it with the proposition that it was "reassuringly expensive".[90] This was used to underwrite the brand and give a base for its positioning, not because it was cheaper but because it was more expensive – a higher price being used to support a higher perceived value. This is as well-known psychological trait known as the "Veblen effect". On the basis of this positioning, carefully maintained over decades, Stella formed perceptions which strongly differentiated it from the rest of the market, and it grew to be the largest alcoholic brand in the UK, with sales of over £500 million a year.

It is noticeable that since Stella abandoned this positioning, it seems to have been floundering. At one point it tried to introduce an extrinsic difference with the promoting of a particular glass which is rather portentously called a "chalice", given that this vessel is usually associated with Christian rituals. Such an innovation might have some peripheral relevance to the on-trade, in bars and restaurants, but it is difficult to see how it could have any direct bearing on those buying it from stores – the majority of its volume. Further to this, Stella then positioned its beer by saying "she is a thing of beauty", which seems rather too self-regarding and narcissistic, not to say arrogant in expecting the consumer to share such aesthetic tastes. In 2016 the brand gave up all together by ditching the promotion of the brand "Stella Artois", which had often been referred to colloquially as just "Stella", and deciding to focus on "Artois". This seemed to indicate an outbreak of schizophrenia absent from the consistent and single-minded message which had so effectively built up the power of the brand over decades of assiduous development. As with the previous case of Microsoft Vista and its vacuous use of the word "wow", nothing is more indicative of the failure of a brand to grasp its basic differentiation than confused and gratuitous advertising.

A more striking example of the mistaken reliance on what the consumer can already see is the creative bankruptcy evident in the used of close-up pack shots in advertising. Perhaps it excites the brand manager to see their pack in all its glory, but it is unlikely that such shots will hold the same fascination for the consumer who does not share a similar obsession with a pack they can regularly admire at the point of sale; they have more important matters. This approach reached its most extreme manifestation when

Pepsi relaunched worldwide with a budget of $500 million in 1996, focusing on a new pack design which it called Big Blue. Its advertising featured shots of the earth dominated by this brave new can, given all the grandeur of a spaceship from *2001: A Space Odyssey*. Yet they appeared to forget that its consumers would have ample time to admire the new can's design in its actual, and more prosaic, setting of the supermarket shelf. It could be argued that the marketing effort would have been better devoted to claiming some perceptual territory, in the way that Jack Daniel's did, rather than telling the consumer something that was staring them in the face. An idea, preferably based on the intrinsic attributes of the brand rather than a statement of the blindingly obvious, tends to have more marketing traction.

5 The power behind words

Because of the potency of differentiation, it is often imagined to have a complexity proportionate to its impact. This is a familiar conceit from which many make a good living by unravelling a supposed spider web which need never have existed in the first place. Often a few words can make all the difference. Joseph Conrad observed, "he who wants to persuade should put his trust not in the right argument but in the right word." As has been mentioned earlier, it is not the words themselves which are powerful, but the concepts behind them; the words are but portals to these. Also what is most easily put into words is not necessarily what is most important. As Iain McGilchrist observed, "a system of thought dependent on language automatically devalues what cannot be expressed in language."[91] In terms of the durability of words themselves, Leonard Mlodinow added that "although we can retain deep structure – the meaning of what was said – for long periods of time, we can accurately remember the surface structure – the words in which it was said – for just eight to 10 seconds."[92]

The crux of the matter was summed up by the nineteenth century Russian political thinker Alexander Herzen. The philosopher Isaiah Berlin wrote that he "grasped, as very few thinkers have ever done, the crucial distinction between words that are about words, and words that are about persons or things in the real world".[93] Advertising is a field where this point often has particular relevance. Frequently there is a resort to puns and analogies, which, while ingenious in terms of the use of words and images, are often merely an end in themselves, paying homage to the verbal or visual dexterity of those who produced the advertisement rather establishing any true differentiation in the real world for the brand itself.

Sometimes the verbal framing of a situation can produce a winning concept. One of the most perceptive was the observation regarding mobile phones that people don't phone places; they phone people. Once the truth of this sinks home, the advantage of mobile phones over fixed landlines is a no-brainer, yet it was debated for long before this – indeed the management consultancy McKinsey famously advised AT&T in 1984 that there was little potential in the mobile market.[94]

Nudge, by Richard Thaler and Cass Sunstein, as noted previously, had international success and spawned a whole area of policy known as "nudge", including what was nicknamed the "Nudge Unit" in the UK government. It is debatable as to whether the book would have had such success or currency if their original title of "Libertarian Paternalism" had been used. When they proposed their work to one publisher, the editor suggested changing the title to *Nudge*, but eventually passed on the book itself. They took the name nonetheless. There was a similar boost for the Brexit campaign to leave the European Union in the UK when they coined the phrase "Vote leave, take control". On a profound level are the terms which are commonly referred to as coming from Charles Darwin's *On the Origin of Species*, particularly "evolution" and "survival of the fittest". Both in fact were coined subsequent to Darwin's book by Herbert Spencer. Darwin himself wrote about "descent with modification" and described how species which adapt to changes in the environment survive, whereas those that do not become extinct, a much more nuanced and reactive development than the assertive individualism inferred by "evolution" and "survival of the fittest". The fact that these terms were subsequently so comprehensively adopted, with even Darwin referring to evolution in later editions, is testimony to the additional power these descriptions conferred on his work, despite the fact that they did not directly reflect it. Words such as those mentioned are described by Robert McKee as "dog whistle words". Like a dog whistle they trigger an almost immediate response.[95]

Another such word is "because". As Robert Cialdini commented, "a well-known principle of human behaviour says that if we ask someone to do us a favour we will be more successful if we provide a reason."[96] He went on to cite a case where the researcher's accomplice wanted to make some photocopies ahead of someone who was already using it. When she asked "I have five pages. May I use the Xerox machine?", on 60 per cent of occasions she was able to do so. But when the question was "I have five pages. May I use the Xerox machine *because* I have to make some copies?", then the number of occasions rose to 90 per cent. In this case, "because" seems to have been a remarkably effective trigger.

The associations of words are also powerful. When researchers added the words "donating = helping" to charity collection boxes, there was a 14 per cent increase in donations over boxes with just information about the appeal. But when "helping" was changed to "loving", as in "donating = loving", the donations increased by more than 90 per cent.[97]

This example obviously has a direct emotional content. But something as emotionally neutral as a number can make a difference, even when it has no direct relevance. In an experiment it was revealed that people were prepared to pay more at a restaurant called Studio 97 than one called Studio 17.[98] In effect, 97 was an anchoring number.

When words are devalued

Words do have potency beyond their mere descriptive role, but it is important to remember that this should always be in the service of differentiation. Often a word is used so much by so many that any effect it has is devalued, and rather than being distinctive it becomes like everyone standing up at a sports stadium for a better view. No advantage is gained in seeing the game, and they might just as well have stayed seated. In food, words such as "natural" suffer from this. In the UK, Mintel, a market research agency, established that one in four new food products had some mention of natural. This company conducted a global study and found that in the last four years, the use of "home-made" in describing new food products had gone up 64 per cent, and "authentic" mentions had risen 80 per cent.[99] It seems misguided to believe that such a currency has any value when it is subjected to such hyperinflation. Any weight as a differentiator is diminished. Pepsi-Cola and Campbell's soup removed "natural" references from their packaging in 2013, given the fact that its extended usage had rendered it increasingly meaningless and certainly of no help in establishing any difference.

Unfortunately the added lustre adjectives can give is often misunderstood, and it appears to be felt that their mere addition will suffice, even if they seem to have no obvious relevance. They can easily end up giving no more meaningful differentiation than the bizarre names which IKEA gives to the items it sells. A good example is an own-label cranberry juice drink in the UK which is described as "bright and bold" – as if anyone ever thought of a juice in these terms let alone in the opposite state of "dull and timid". Such use of words just to fill in space results in vacuous piffle.

Mistaking the form of a word for its substance

The nature of words as merely the currency of thought has been mentioned. A good illustration of how money depends on what is behind it in terms of agreed value is provided by the inhabitants of the Pacific island of Yap. They had a monetary system based on stone discs called "Fei", measuring up to twelve feet in diameter. They were so unwieldy they were rarely moved but could change ownership without ever physically changing hands – one of the stones being left lying on the seabed after a shipwreck. In the same way that currency such as the Fei is merely a portal to credit, so words are portals to thought. To think of them as having value in themselves is equivalent to the pointless exercise of diving for the Fei at the bottom of the sea, as opposed to using it for its agreed purpose.

Unfortunately the truth of this observation is often lost sight of when brands try to differentiate themselves, not just by the words themselves but by the letters that compose them – taking the brand to two removes from reality. This appears to be a search for differentiation based on a fatuous belief that individual letters are dice to be juggled and thrown to give a winning combination. Such blinkered thinking has resulted in many empty campaigns which seem to be based on the misleading premise of awareness as an end in itself, rather than the application of thought regarding what the message is that is communicated to consumers and whether it resonates with them.

A particularly glaring example of this was HTC mobile phones. A global advertising campaign was introduced with great fanfare and great expenditure. Yet it was built on the red herring of pointless, self-indulgent speculation as to what the acronym HTC stood for. Various absurd suggestions were put forward, such as Humongous Tinfoil Catamaran, Hipster Troll Carwash, Hot Tea Catapult, Happy Telephone Company and Hold This Cat. It is difficult to comprehend what this was supposed to say about HTC, other than it didn't have a clue as to what its name stood for. Maybe they felt that this game of speculation was something which would intrigue consumers? Unfortunately people are never as interested in arcane aspects of a brand name as those working for the brand. If kicking a can down the road is a way of differentiating, then this might be deemed a success. It isn't.

This rather empty approach to advertising and differentiation was later compounded by a subsequent campaign for the HTC One mobile, which started from the cod philosophical base of "we're all one" and segued this into a pun on the brand's name. What this had to say about how the brand was different it is impossible to say. But it had a lot to say about the global marketing director of HTC. He described the evolution of the campaign:

> We hired the world's most expensive, most popular star, Robert Downey Jr. And then I called him. "You're going to have to help us." . . . In the studio, I said, "I don't want to show your face." He said, "Oh, great." We don't want the view that we're trying to commoditize an artist. It's not a celebrity endorsement. Somehow, I don't know why, it happened in the past – it feels like someone paying him to say something. It never works. It's not like we're selling beer or whiskey. So, we create a story. It's so poetic. It's very, very different. Nothing fancy. Just to tell our story.[100]

This star-struck piffle could be a great comedy sketch, but it was all too real. This folly was advanced even further by the fact that the company had Robert Downey Jr. contribute to the writing of the ads.

How any of these exercises contributed to giving the brand a solid differentiation is impossible to speculate, as few elements were offered for serious thought. In 2011 HTC's share of all smartphones sold in the world peaked at 10.7 per cent, a figure that has since slid to around 3 per cent according to projections by mobile device analysts.[101] There is one area where the supposed differentiation of HTC advertising is helpful: in answering the dilemma of John Wanamaker, an American department-store magnate, who is reported to have said that "I know half my advertising doesn't work, I just don't know which half." At least HTC provided a clear answer to this – most likely none of it.

In Napa Valley, the centre of the US wine industry, nearly every wine producer refers to themselves as a "family" winery or vineyard. It seems unlikely that this gives them any differentiation when they all use it. "Family" is a word which has connotations of an intimate social unit, so it is unclear how it can have any relevance to large commercial operations other than giving a generic emotional platform which has nothing to do with the intrinsic properties of the brand. The extent of the divorce from its actual meaning is summarised by Gallo wines, owner of the two biggest wine brands in the world, who describe themselves as "Gallo Family Vineyards". It seems rather fanciful to imagine that such a behemoth might be viewed as an intimate unit; therefore the use of the term "family" in this particular context seems inappropriate and misleading.

Unfortunately the use of words is often lazy and without any real understanding of their import. A good example of this was the way a 50 cl bottle of wine was described by a supermarket in the UK. The reason for this size was that the most frequent occasion for drinking wine was at home with a person's partner, wife or husband, accounting for nearly 40 per cent of the times when wine was drunk. Consequently the 50 cl size was called "Vin a Deux: The Comfortable Size for Two" to appeal directly to this rather large segment. Unfortunately when it was launched, the supermarket announced it as "Wines from across France for you and a friend". The reference to France was redundant, as there was no point of difference in wines coming from France – many wines do! Also the use of the word "friend" was divorced from the intended context of the size, as most people tend to have drinks with a friend away from home in a wine bar or pub and usually there might be more than just one friend on these occasions, whereas the home situation, which was the appropriate context, is with a partner, husband or wife – an altogether more intimate and significant occasion than with a friend and one in which there were just two participants. No other wine size catered to this specific target, so this point of difference was lost due to the failure to apply the simplest thinking, an omission too often apparent in marketing as well as many other fields. The advertising legend David Ogilvy said that the two most important words in advertising were "free" and "new". The 50 cl size for mainstream wines was undoubtedly new, but no mention was made of this defining differentiator.

A simple turn of phrase can differentiate a brand and give it a unique position. The same is true of a person. One of the first impressions Barack Obama made on a wider audience was his speech at the Democratic Convention in 2004, when he proclaimed, "there are no red states, no blue states, just united states" (red being the colour for Republicans and blue for Democrats). As Matthew Barzun, US ambassador to the UK, stated, "My distinctive memory of that speech wasn't thinking at all. It was feeling. A feeling more than a thought."[102] He then went on to point out that this was always the first thing to come out in focus groups regarding Obama. It became a positive point of differentiation.

This helped in terms of establishing the authority of Obama. But there is a tendency for people to accept messages when framed in the guise of an authoritative figure; in this case authority becomes the differentiator. As Daniel Kanheman observed, "people are not accustomed to thinking hard and are often content to trust a plausible judgement that quickly comes to mind".[103] Obviously the plausible differentiation conferred by an authority is a welcome relief from such a tiresome task as thinking, as mentioned in the previous example regarding how people delegate evaluation to experts. In an experiment, 95 per cent of nurses obeyed instructions from someone who announced himself as a physician but whom they did not know. As was wryly observed, the "experiment strongly suggests, however, that one of these intelligentsias (nurses vs. physicians) is, for all practical purposes, non-functioning".[104] The power inferred by authority as a differentiator was also evident in an experiment whereby people were told, "He's overparked but doesn't have any change. Give him a dime." When the person in question was dressed as a security guard, 92 per cent obliged, but when dressed normally, only 42 per cent did.[105]

Words are also used by many professions which seek to distinguish themselves by the use of arcane language such as that of lawyers in the UK, whereby a meeting is a "conference". In the 1930s Marvin Bower of McKinsey decided to try to make consultants as well-regarded as other professions by developing their own particular vocabulary, whereby a business was a "practice", a customer was a "client", employees were "firm members" and negotiating was termed as "making arrangements".[106]

Serendipitous encounters are often the source for simple yet effective differentiation through words. Audi in the UK had a very successful advertising campaign over many years, which positioned it firmly as a premium car brand. One of the foundations of this was the phrase "Vorsprung durch Technik", which has since been used throughout the world, except for the

United States. As Sir John Hegarty, the creative director of Audi's agency Bartle, Bogle, Hegarty recounted,

> I had gone to Ingolstadt and found the factory and I saw a very old faded poster on the wall that someone had left up there . . . I saw this line "Vorsprung durch Technik". They said that was an old advertising line but "we don't use it any more". And it stuck in my brain.[107]

He had no idea what it actually meant ("progress through technology"), but once he'd been told, the idea remained. "This is the incidental nature of creativity, looking, watching, hearing stuff and it all goes in." Later, when the agency was looking for a line to tie all the advertising work together, the phrase came back. "Everyone looked at me as though I was mad," said Hegarty. No one really used foreign languages to advertise in those days. But the client went with it, and soon it was a catchphrase of mid-1980s Britain.

"It was the first time, certainly, that a foreign phrase captured the public's imagination in that way," Hegarty recalled. "There was a history [with Germany]. There was the possibility of rubbing people up the wrong way, but it's amazing how it took off and how it became a part of British culture." Within a few short years the phrase had featured in songs by Blur and U2, the movie *Lock, Stock and Two Smoking Barrels* and in an episode of a popular British comedy series called *Only Fools and Horses*.

Even just a simple change of name can make a massive change, and it can cost nothing. The story of the humble Pilchard in the UK illustrates this. It was a fish with poor PR; indeed the name was toxic. Pilchards had been perceived as being almost in the same category as Spam luncheon meat. Yet there were bountiful supplies off the southwest coast of England, around Cornwall. Nick Howell, manager of the Pilchard Works factory and museum at Newlyn, wanted to change this dire situation and noted that the Pilchard was in fact a member of the Sardine family, only a little larger than other varieties. He came up with the name "Cornish Sardine" – a name which was an invention but was clearly an accurate description of the fish and so remained true to its intrinsic qualities.

In 1997 the average price paid to fishermen for a landed kilo of "Pilchards" had been £0.015, and the total catch came in at seven tons. By 2003 the average price paid for a kilo of "Cornish Sardines" – the very same fish – was £1.00.[108] By 2008 the quantity landed was 1,596 tons. The reality had not changed, just the perception based on a simple change of name. This position was further reinforced when, in 2009, Cornish Sardines were given protected name status by the EU. The status was awarded to them because of the way the fish are caught and the historical link to sardine fishing in

Cornish waters.[109] A name change which was barely 10 years old acquired an historical heritage and an assured differentiation.

A rather simpler example of the nudge effect of a new name comes from sport. The London Community Cricket Association was a charity set up in London after inner-city riots in 1981. Its purpose was to develop projects aimed at getting unemployed and directionless young people to train as cricket coaches. It then changed its name to Cricket for Change, and without any other variations, the contributions rose from £200,000 p.a. to £600,000 p.a. in three years.

Sometimes a word itself can be a real danger and have a toxic effect of its own, as is the case with leprosy. Brazil is one of the two countries in the world with the highest incidence of this disease. The very word is one which is likely to induce the most profound fear and panic, given the baggage associated with leprosy. But the disease can now be treated relatively easily, with antibiotics. Such an advance has not yet overcome perceptions. Consequently, to avoid the emotional trauma associated with the word, the Brazilian government has ceased to use it and now calls leprosy Hansen's disease, after the nineteenth century Danish doctor who identified the cause of leprosy. So now, when someone has a skin complaint, it is identified by this name and treated accordingly, with far less fuss and hysterics that the word leprosy would have triggered.

More specific = more compelling

In terms of the nature of the story, Kahneman pointed out that a rich and vivid representation encourages people to have more faith in what it is describing. The simple example he used gave two choices:

1. A 21 per cent chance to receive $59 next Monday
2. A 21 per cent chance to receive a large blue cardboard envelope containing $59 next Monday morning

His hypothesis was that the individual would be more likely to opt for the second option, despite the fact that the probability of both outcomes was the same. This was because the blue envelope evokes a richer and more fluent representation than the abstract notion of a sum of money. The richer image tends to construct a more rooted reality, as the more specific a description, the more arresting the image.

Kahneman and Tversky explored the effect of being more specific in an experiment. They told their respondents that they had picked a person from a pool of 100 people, 70 of whom were engineers and 30 of whom were lawyers. When they were asked what was the likelihood of a person selected being a lawyer, they correctly stated it was 30 per cent. There was another pool consisting of 70 lawyers and 30 engineers, and they the correctly stated that there was a 70 per cent chance of the person plucked from the pool being a lawyer. Then they were told that it was not a nameless person who had been picked but someone called Dick and they were read a description of Dick, which contained no information to help the respondent guess what Dick did for a living. They then guessed that there was an equal chance that Dick was a lawyer or an engineer, no matter what pool he came from. As Kahneman and Tversky commented: "when no specific evidence is given, the prior probabilities are properly utilised; when worthless specific evidence is given, prior probabilities are ignored."[110]

Specificity also makes it more difficult to overlook the message, as evidenced by the book *The Terrible Secret: Suppression of the Truth about Hitler's "Final Solution"* by Walter Laqueur. Jon Elster explains that, in this case, the lack of specific knowledge may make the general knowledge more possible to bear. Many Germans thought Jews were no longer alive but did not necessarily believe that they were dead. This failure to draw the logical conclusion from their own beliefs partly resulted from lack of specific information that they were actually dead; in effect their conscience was left some wiggle room.[111]

As Max Muller commented, "there is no such thing as a tree, but only this or that fir tree or oak tree or apple tree . . . Tree, therefore is a concept and, as such, can never be seen or perceived by the senses."[112] A specific description gives something solid to hold on to; otherwise there is a tendency to the vacuous. In marketing terms this is well illustrated by Sherry in the UK. It is a word which has strong negatives in terms of perceptions and is thought of as something slightly sweet, drunk by one's maiden aunt. There is also the emotional irony that the dowdy image of Sherry is oblivious to the fact that an intrinsic aspect of its region is the passion and dynamism of flamenco – the opposite of what the word "Sherry" conjures up. The use of the word Sherry is almost as generic as that of "tree" in the observation of Muller – for the term applies to the wines of the region of Jerez in Spain, which has the widest range of wines of any region, covering the whole spectrum from very dry to very sweet. Also the biggest and most dynamic category is the dry Finos and Manzanillas which, because of the name Sherry, are tarred with the brush of being sweet and dowdy. Being specific about these wines and representing them solely by their actual names can lead to the approach Steve Jobs adopted for the Intel chip, mentioned previously. A liberal interpretation could be "Starting today, Fino and Manzanilla will be set free from the toxic associations with the sweetness and frumpiness of Sherry. Imagine the possibilities."

The seeming reluctance to focus on the specific is clearly illustrated by much copy in marketing, which may sound nice but actually says little to give a clear differentiation from competition through the intrinsic merits of the brand. An area where this is particularly apparent is the clear opportunity provided by labels on wine bottles, which is usually squandered. A good example of this is the positioning and label on Tio Pepe Sherry, the biggest Fino brand. The current front label and back and copy are as follows:

TIO PEPE

JEREZ, XERES, SHERRY

Fino Muy Seco

For more than 150 years the uncompromising dryness of Tio Pepe has been appreciated by wine lovers around the world. Refreshing and distinctive, Tio Pepe is a wine for all occasions and is the perfect partner for fish, shellfish, cheese and white meats, and "tapas" of course. Drink it straight or on ice. Always serve chilled, refrigerate after opening and enjoy within a month.

This communicates little that is intrinsic and different about Tio Pepe and is similar to many other wine labels, which appear as rather fine verbal vessels, but with little content of any substance. Ironically the wine industry has already been noted as one which has little appreciation of the power of marketing. This is only confirmed by such a hollow exercise.

Such an omission is unfortunate when the brand can tap into a strong intrinsic story and position stated in equally brief terms:

TIO PEPE

The First in Fino

In 1835 Manuel Maria Gonzalez started the company that became Gonzalez Byass. Fino was then only drunk locally in Jerez. Manuel's uncle, Pepe, suggested that he should be the first to make it for a wider audience. It was a big success and others followed. In gratitude, Manuel named it after Pepe, "tio" being Spanish for uncle.

Tio Pepe is suitable for any occasion. It is perfect with fish, shellfish, cured meats, white meats and tapas. Always serve chilled, straight or on ice. Refrigerate after opening and enjoy within a month.

It is up to the reader to decide which is the more potent of these two messages. Hopefully it will be noted that the second is more specific and less generic and so gains extra leverage from this.

There is also evidence that flowery metaphors which are relevant, such as "crispy cucumbers" and "velvety mashed potatoes" tempt people to order food which is more richly described and even lead them to rate those foods as tasting better than the identical foods given only a generic description.[113] As Aristotle observed in the *Poetics*, poetry is better if its mode is dramatic rather than narrative.

This was added to by Antonio Damasio, who noted that research had indicated that if you told stories of comparable length with a comparable number of facts, differing only in that in one the facts had a high emotional content, then you will remember far more detail from the emotional story than from the factual one.[114]

This is true of the writing that describes a difference. Often there is a tendency to get lost in florid language, which sounds impressive but then evaporates and reveals itself to offer nothing more substantial than the plumage of a peacock. To continue with the natural analogy, a snowflake is alluring in its perfection, and each one is unique. But it is important to note that its starting point is a speck of dust which is all too real and mundane. All its intricacy is based on this particle, without which the snowflake would not form. So too with the description of a brand's difference, it needs to have something of substance at its core, which can serve as solid foundations for the brand's uniqueness.

When exploiting such facts, it would seem obvious that they need to mean something to the consumer. Unfortunately, this is often not the case, and the person writing forgets that they are not writing for themselves but for consumers. One of the most prominent examples of this lack of empathy is the wine industry, whose members appear to be so pleased by their verbalisation of taste, however arcane, that they insist on subjecting the consumer to it. This leads to descriptions which are vain articulations well beyond the world of the consumer and appear to be written only for the writers and their colleagues in the industry. One such was a description of a particular wine as having "the scent of Garrigue". This is meaningless to 99.9 per cent of the market and not even present in a French dictionary. After much investigation, it eventually turned out to be a bush which grows in the Provence region of southern France. No doubt the ego of the writer was served, but alas not the understanding of the consumer. In this particular case it is interesting to note that the person at the supermarket involved explained the acceptance of this description was due to the fact that it was written by a wine critic. It is difficult to grasp how this illustrious source countered the bemusement of the consumer. This is another example of the blind acceptance of the so-called expert and the abandonment of common sense.

Such facts which are chosen need to have potency, but often, in order to have a solid foundation, they need to follow what Ernest Hemingway called the "iceberg theory", whereby a writer needed to know everything about a subject, even if the vast majority of that knowledge remains submerged. This was also evident in a talk given by Jeremy Herrin and Denise Gough, the director and principal actress in *People, Places and Things*, an acclaimed theatrical production in London. They constructed backstories for all the characters, even though these details were never mentioned in the play. This gave a more solid foundation and added depth to these individuals. The English novelist Tim Lott attended a seminar given by Robert McKee, about which he noted, "'everything is subtext', I wrote. This is really what McKee teaches above all else – that the best drama will always happen below the surface."[115]

6 Visual differentiation

Simple visual differentiation can make a big difference, particularly given the emphasis which people give to images. The Visual Social Media Lab in Sheffield in the UK was founded in 2014 when they recorded that worldwide five hundred million images a day were being shared. By the summer of 2016, this had risen to four billion.[116] Farida Vis of the Lab gave a poignant example of the effect of one image, the 2015 photo of Alan Kurdi, the drowned three-year old Syrian refugee. She noted that every single interviewee she spoke to had seen this image. It made a difference; in September 2015 the research for refugee-related issues on Google was the highest in history. Also, newspapers which had previously referred to refugees as cockroaches suddenly became sympathetic. She felt that part of the effect of the picture was that is symbolised one story rather than a mass. Normally reports on refugees had featured photos of crowds, and as she observed, "it is difficult to create empathy when the dominant image is a mass of people".

A rather lighter example occurred in the village of Borja in Spain. In 2012 an amateur art restorer, eighty-year-old Cecilia Giménez, tried to restore a fading fresco of Jesus Christ called "Ecce Homo" ("Behold the Man"). But the result was unrecognisable. The new painting was a botched job. It was so bad that, since its completion, it attracted more than 160,000 visitors to the church, dwarfing the 5,000 population of the village. There are "Ecce Homo" souvenirs, from pens ($2) to mugs ($7) to wine featuring Jesus's tragically altered face on the label (approximately $4 to $11 a bottle).[117] In 2016 a centre was opened dedicated to this picture. It was certainly different.

There is also the fact that visual differentiation can often override any verbal message, even if rationally it is felt that the latter is the driver. This was well illustrated in the 1980s when President Reagan cut funding to children with disabilities and opposed funding for public health schemes.

His visit to a nursing home and attendance at the Special Olympics struck TV journalist Lesley Stahl as a level of hypocrisy that needed to be exposed. She thought she had done this via a report spanning more than five minutes. But she was apprehensive as to what the reaction would be from the White House, feeling she might be blacklisted. To her amazement a senior member of Reagan's staff congratulated her. When she expressed surprise, they pointed out that "nobody heard what you said . . . when the pictures are powerful and emotional, they override, if not completely drown out, the sound."[118]

Another example of the overriding effect of the visual was again provided by Reagan. He was hardly a champion of the environment, and most of his statements on it had a distinctly off-green tinge. Yet whenever he made them, he would be pictured sitting on a horse in an open-necked shirt, somewhere out west. His visual context was the environment, even though the message was not. As previously observed, given that most people do not listen to what is said, the message they took away was of someone in synch with nature.

Politics is a rich field for visual differentiation. Some researchers in California created campaign flyers for several fictional congressional elections. Half the models chosen for the photos looked able and competent; the other half did not look quite so gifted. When it came to selection by the respondents, those candidates with the better demeanour won, on average, 59 per cent of the vote.[119] In modern politics that is considered a landslide; the only American president to have won by such a margin since the Great Depression was Lyndon Johnson, who beat Barry Goldwater with 61 per cent of the vote in 1964.

In addition to overall concepts, there is the visual nature of the brand which can provide differentiation. A logo can clearly signal differentiation, not for what it is itself but for what it signifies as a direct portal for perceptions about the particular brand. Iain McGilchrist pointed out that we process words serially, whereas a visual image is taken in all at once and tends to summarise the *gestalt* of the particular thing it represents.[120] So a logo can be a more powerful differentiator than a word. Just think of what lies behind a viewing of the Nike swoosh or the Johnny Walker walking man – much more distinctive and richer than simply the writing of the name. In addition the existence of a strong logo representing the brand gives licence to a double whammy of being able to use the brand's tag line in conjunction, such as "Just do it" with the Nike swoosh or "Keep walking" with the Johnny Walker man. By contrast, the use of these lines with the written name of the brands would appear clumsy and superfluous.

Visual appearance, together with customer usability, was at the heart of the extraordinary success of Apple. In his marketing philosophy for Apple, Mike Markkula stated:

> We may have the best product, the highest quality, the most useful software, etc. If we present them in a slipshod manner they will be perceived as slipshod; if we present them in a creative and professional manner we will impute the desired qualities.[121]

For Markkula, you could judge a book by its cover. This approach was also echoed in the approach of the designer for the early Apple computers, Hartmut Esslinger of Frog design, whom Steve Jobs went to because of his iconic design work for the Sony Trinitron TV. Esslinger's guiding principle was "form follows emotion", and he proposed a "born-in-America gene for Apple's DNA",[122] aiming for differentiation in design based on Apple's American roots. For Jobs, design was essential as a differentiator. He commented that "in most people's vocabularies design means veneer. But to me nothing could be further from the meaning of design. Design is the fundamental soul of a man-made creation that ends up expressing itself in successive outer layers."[123]

It is tempting to see the success of Apple as being due to product innovation, which is true of some features, whereas the truth is more to do with design. Their great successes were the iPod, iPhone and iPad. Yet these were all products which had already existed for some time, in the shape of the MP3 player, the smartphone and the tablet computer, which was, as has been mentioned, already being developed by Microsoft. Apple's designs differentiated their versions of these products to the extent that the iPhone has sold a billion units since its introduction in 2007 and is the most successful consumer product ever, generating almost $625bn (£475bn) in revenue in just nine years. It was the main driver for Apple becoming the largest company in the world in terms of market capitalisation.

Another example is the Benson and Hedges cigarette pack, which had a slide pack with a drawer incorporated in the design of the pack, a feature unique to this brand. Japan Tobacco International, the owner of the brand, credited this innovation with a 47 per cent increase in sales in one year.[124]

The opposite effect in terms of visual differentiation was achieved in Canada. The government started using pictures of rotting teeth, cancerous lungs and damaged brains and hearts to make the consequences of smoking visually apparent. Regulations required 50 per cent of the packs to feature these images. Research showed that these were sixty times more likely to persuade smokers to quit than text-only warnings.[125]

The visual can influence even through the very font in which words are set. A study was conducted on the effects of different fonts on attitudes toward preparing food. Participants were asked to read a recipe for making a Japanese dish and to rate the amount of effort and skill they thought the recipe would require and how likely they would be to make the dish at home. Those who were presented with the recipe in a difficult-to-read font regarded it as more difficult and said they were less likely to make the dish. This approach was repeated with a one-page description of an exercise regime, and again respondents said that they were less likely to follow the instructions when they were written in the more difficult font. Such outcomes are due to what psychologists call the "fluency effect". When the *form* of the information is difficult to assimilate, it affects judgement about the *substance* of the information.[126]

The self-seduction of ads

Often when people talk about ads they appear to regard them as a point of differentiation in themselves rather than a means of communicating a particular message. Invariably they are considered in the same light as a movie, with admiration expressed for the cinematic qualities rather than the idea behind them. There is no doubt that the viewer, like the originator, can be seduced by the visual qualities of the film. But these can only serve as a very flimsy base for differentiation. They are like the snowflake referred to previously, except that they do not have the speck of dust as a foundation; they have no idea behind them. It is a little like the obsession with words alone rather than the concept which they convey. This can often end up with the advertising representing an extrinsic aspect, rather than it being held accountable for its main purpose, which is to focus on the intrinsic.

This is often true of advertisements that amaze and captivate the viewer with their creativity. They are rightly admired, just as many movies are praised. Yet there is a crucial difference: films are there to entertain; advertisements are there to promote a brand. This is frequently forgotten, leading to ads being appreciated only as creative expressions. Unfortunately, this cinematic excellence is so seductive that it can obscure the absence of a solid idea which could serve as the base for engagement. An example of a cinematic "shock and awe" approach is the glorious advertisement for the Apple Macintosh in 1984, playing on the theme of George Orwell's novel *1984* and directed by Ridley Scott. This is often regarded as one of the greatest ads ever made. It finished with the line, "On January 24th Apple Computer will introduce the Macintosh and you'll see why 1984 won't be like '1984'". It was only aired once, and a year later the Macintosh was only achieving a quarter of its sales target; the previous Apple III model sustained the company. There was no differentiation, but reliance was placed on visual fireworks and a portentous statement which was, on even the most cursory assessment, totally vacuous.

Similar awe is also expressed for a Guinness ad featuring white horses and a surfer. It is stunning but, on inspection, seems to do little to establish the idea of "good things come to those who wait" which was supposedly its raison d'être. There was no clear establishment of waiting, and it is difficult to see how the wonderful spectacle of the white horses did anything for the surfing experience of the surfer, as opposed to the viewer's visual excitement. The "good thing" which is central to the concept is difficult to gauge from the surfer's point of view, as he seems to have little involvement – this being the province of the white horses. Once a wave crashes, there is little that remains, so too with any solid idea being left by this ad.

Obsession with the ads themselves can reach vacuous proportions, such as demonstrated by a trade magazine called the Drinks Business which had a collection of "cool" beer ads with the comment "beer companies have always been forced to go the extra mile to not only build their brand but ensure their customers maintain that loyalty through eye-catching TV ads". Again the tenor of the comment is akin to someone seeing a film at the cinema. How building a brand and maintaining loyalty is to be achieved by tinsel is not explained.

The role of the advertising should not be to stun visually. That can help, but the differentiation of the brand should have a more solid base than "shock and awe" – an empty and unsustaining platform. Despite having a visual eloquence which might produce awe at the time, without the underpinning of an idea, as with verbal rhetoric, it can soon evaporate or signify nothing other than itself, when its sole reason should be the underwriting of the brand. This is often forgotten.

Donald Norman defined good designs as "those which fit our needs so well that the design is invisible, serving us without drawing attention to itself".[127] The same can apply to marketing. There are parallels in an ad, as it should not necessarily draw attention to itself but hopefully convey a point of differentiation which is so clear and engaging that it does not have to shout. Heath and Hyder illustrated this when questioning the importance of awareness in the case of Stella Artois, which has already been commented on as the most successful beer brand in the UK.[128] Despite having run for eight years, Stella's initial press campaign (as measured by a competitor's tracking study) had only achieved claimed ad awareness of 4 per cent in 1990, compared with 29 per cent for the leading TV advertised brand, Castlemaine XXXX. Yet Stella's rating for quality on the same survey was 45 per cent, compared with just 19 per cent for Castlemaine. A rigorous analysis of all other factors indicated that it could only have been the advertising which gave the brand its exceptionally high reputation, thereby indicating that advertising can build strong brand values without shouting. This was underwritten by Norman in his comments on design, saying that "the design challenge is to present information about the state of the system in a way that is easy to assimilate and interpret."[129]

Interestingly part of the success of Stella Artois was built on the differentiation provided by the ads themselves. Given that its category was lager, most advertising in the UK aimed at this sector tended to focus on a "lads" approach, a quirky and whacky style which was intended to appeal to the young male consumers who were the primary target. In contrast Stella produced ads which had a distinct cultural bias, being initially based on the style of the French film *Jeanne de Florette*, set in Provence. Also they were always in French, to underwrite their difference. Yet they never strayed from the central idea of "reassuringly expensive".

7   Differentiation comes in many forms

In marketing, as in many other fields, serendipity often plays a key role. By its nature it cannot be factored into any consideration, but it is something of which the participants need to be aware. Often differentiation can turn on seemingly frivolous and superficial points but, as they can play a crucial role in distinguishing one offer from another, they then need to be recognised for the leverage they can provide.

One such point was in the field of architecture. Norman Foster is one of the most prominent architects of his generation and is world famous, having worked on many iconic buildings, from the British Museum to the Reichstag; he has also designed major buildings such as Hong Kong airport. His first major commission was for the offices of an insurance company, Willis Faber Dumas, in Ipswich south-east England. This was a revolutionary building. At a celebration for an anniversary of these offices, the chartered surveyor for the project said he had asked the chairman of the company why he had chosen Foster from the other contestants for the project. "I liked the way they dressed" was the reply. This might seem flippant, but for the fact that it was true and vital. Although the design of the building has been lauded over the years, it was the dress sense of Foster and his associates which actually won on the day and was the crucial differentiator.

This illustrates well the perspective of Theodore Levitt. For him, nothing was a commodity; everything could be found to have some aspect which provided differentiation. He observed that "everybody – whether producer, fabricator, seller, broker, agent, merchant – engages in a constant effort to distinguish his offering in his favour from all others".[130] He went on to observe that "the usual presumption about so-called undifferentiated commodities is that they are exceedingly price sensitive. That's seldom true, except in the imaginary world of economic textbooks."[131] Even iron ore, which is thought by many as an ultimate example of a commodity, Levitt pointed out could be differentiated. This could be achieved not just through technical specifications of the particular ore, but also through the level of service from a particular company in its provision. As there was often no other point of differentiation, then this particular aspect of service took on a role which was decisive. In the case of Foster, it was a differentiation of which he himself was probably not aware.

The range of options for achieving differentiation was one area which was not fully appreciated by Henry Ford. His main obsession was a rather blinkered one with price and the product. The Model T Ford fell in price from $825 in 1908 to $290 in 1927. Yet although two million were sold in 1923, by 1926 sales had fallen to 1.5 million. The reason for this was that a whole range of other differentiators was introduced by Ford's main competition General Motors under Alfred P. Sloan which, by 1927, was selling 1.8 million cars. Henry Ford had a horror of debt which allowed his competitors to gain advantage through differentiating by new forms of payment, such as accepting credit and paying by instalments. Sloan priced Chevrolet at $450–$600, which he described as "taking a bite from the top of his position" and was justified by the extras offered. He also introduced the idea of new models each year. Sloan knew Ford would stick with the lower prices and was content to leave that sector to him.[132] Although the added features helped in GM's case, this is an area which needs to be treated with caution, as will be explored later.

Differentiation through service is intangible but obviously important for service brands. With Purolator Courier in Canada, the differentiator became the time of day. The top companies were seen as similar in satisfying the core needs of consumers, and thus any differentiation was difficult. Purolator's research had identified the 9 a.m. Day Starter service as their product with the most potential. It demonstrated that Purolator put the consumer first by responding to and anticipating their needs. The basis for this strategy came from psychology and the concept of the circadian rhythms of the body. This focused on the patterns the body goes through each day, and some studies had shown that a person's productivity decreases as the day advances. Also, from a purely intuitive viewpoint, it was hypothesised that with the advance of the day, a person's stress levels would rise and their feelings of control would slip away. Consumers agreed with this.

Consequently, for the senders, the 9 a.m. arrival meant that their package would get undivided attention, and for the receivers there was a window to focus on its contents before things got out of control or, as Purolator put it, "before the day got to them". They were then able to build on the commitment and leadership that Day Start demonstrated to potential customers. Day Start increased in volume by 27 per cent within a year and helped raise the overall business of Purolator by 10 per cent.[133]

Taking a product generic and claiming it for your brand

Although great emphasis has been put on the intrinsic, this is not to say that a particular aspect needs to be unique to the brand but rather that the strength of the brand's claim to it makes it so. Often there are intrinsic generic product qualities which can be claimed for a brand to the exclusion of others by what is, in effect, a pre-emptive strike. Any of the brands in a market could have alighted on a particular point, but once one brand has claimed it, then it becomes that brand's property and so, in the eyes of the consumer, it is differentiated from the other brands, even though they could quite legitimately have made the same claim. Such a move has all the elegance of a checkmate in chess and can be equally effective.

Unfortunately there are many instances when the generic is so well known by those in the industry that they assume the consumer is similarly knowledgeable and thus miss an opportunity. This was evident in the description of "trafilata al bronzo", which some Italian pasta brands have on their packs. Even if it had been translated into English, it would have had little significance. This means that the pasta is extruded through bronze dies. But what is not explained, given the blinkered assumption that consumers already knew, is that using bronze results in the pasta having a more textured surface which is better for holding the sauce. One of the leading brands, De Cecco, featured it and then removed it. This was understandable as, given they had never explained it, the term was meaningless. The alternative to bronze dies are Teflon ones, which are often used. They produce pasta with a smoother surface, which makes it more difficult for the sauce to stick. Consequently, seizing the production generic of the bronze die could result in it being associated with the brand which laid claim to it first and thus provide differentiation.

The potential of this point of difference was finally recognised by Napolina when they launched their Bronze Die range. Through the copy on the pack they explained to the consumer how the pasta was: "Extruded through traditional 'bronze dies' creating a textured pasta with a rough surface, allowing sauces to stick for a fuller flavour". This aspect of holding the sauce was mentioned by several of the customer reviews on the delivery service Ocado's website as something which had been noticed and appreciated.[134] Given that this had seldom been stated before as a criterion for pasta, it seems probable that the thought had been introduced by Napolina – the only brand to seize this as a point of differentiation.

Napolina chose to make its bronze die range a premium one, with linguine selling at £1.99 for 500 gms as opposed to £1.20 for the standard range. De Cecco, which had abandoned any thought of using this differentiator, usually has a retail price of £1.55 for its linguine, but this is often discounted to

£1.00. Napolina states that this range is successful in the market, and given the figures, it might be deduced that this is particularly true of the margins – changing a die being a low level increase in costs. Napolina simply took something that was generic in the industry, made it their own and explained its benefit to consumers. Through this they established a meaningful competitive advantage with a simple point of differentiation.

Fortunately there are cases when the generic is firmly taken, as was true of the bid for the 2012 Olympics. There were five contenders: Madrid, Paris, New York, Moscow and London. The first four paraded a list of clichéd stereotypes: flamenco dancers, romantic French music, multi-ethnicity and the Russian bear. In contrast the London bid barely mentioned London, except as inspiration for the theme they chose: "London's vision is to reach young people all around the world, so that they are inspired to choose sport." Their film for the bid was not a city travelogue, but featured African kids in shanty towns; a Latin American boy seeing a cycling race and jumping on his own bike; and a Russian girl, transfixed by swimming on TV, who decides to start training. The idea was that behind every child there is a potential Olympic hero and that sport transforms the world.

As David Magliano, director of the marketing bid for the London Olympics noted, "we were not the only ones who could tell the story of how the Games could inspire young people to choose sport, but we were the only ones who did tell that story".[135] The whole approach was summed up by the closing speeches of the Paris and London bids. The former stated "Paris wants the games, Paris needs the games, Paris loves the games", whereas London pitched its tent on higher moral ground: "On behalf of the youth of today, the athletes of tomorrow and the Olympians of the future, we humbly submit the bid of London 2012."

Sometimes the claiming of a generic requires a little finesse, even in such a prosaic market as instant noodles. In the UK Batchelors Supernoodles were stuck in the traditional kids' teatime usage occasion. They had discovered some young adult users who made up for their relatively small numbers by the large quantities they consumed. For them, "filling up" was the objective and Supernoodles were seen as quick, satisfying and moreish.

This segment of the market was called "the substantial snacking sector", but the consumers themselves called it "foody nosh". Bachelors chose to own it, although it was open to all, being a characteristic of every product in the market. They achieved this by using the description "great foody nosh" for their Supernoodles. Weekly sales during the advertising of this position rose by 72 per cent, and production couldn't keep up with the demand. Also Supernoodles' overall share of the market rose from around 59–65 per cent to 77 per cent with the first burst of advertising and 84 per cent with the second. Given Supernoodles' dominant position in the market, there was also an increase in its overall size of 14 per cent.[136]

Getting up close and personal

Supernoodles was building on a position of dominance, while in Australia Listerine mouthwash was trying to recover past glories. It had been the first mouthwash on the market and initially had the whole category to itself but had then slid to a share low of 23.6 per cent. It further had the negative of an unpleasant strong taste, which was felt to be too much for consumers' needs.

This led to Listerine claiming that all mouthwashes freshened breath but only Listerine killed the germs that caused bad breath and other oral problems. The strong taste was part of the proof. Sales doubled in three and a half years, and profits rose by 80 per cent.

... Or just very personal

Another product with a personal aspect is women's sanitary napkins. Procter and Gamble's (P&G) Always was the most successful feminine care brand in the world, with a global worth of over $2 billion and over 50 per cent of the market in many countries. It dominated the developed markets, but in emerging ones its premium position limited its potential, as these were markets where the cheaper brands dominated. To address this situation they had launched an inexpensive soft pad called Always Classic which tested well against competition. However it failed to achieve a satisfactory share and suffered from the additional problem that a significant proportion of its sales cannibalised other Always variants.

In response to this P&G decided to develop a new brand. The basis of the company's marketing had historically centred around establishing a significant product advantage for its brands. However, commercial analysis made it clear that for this new brand there was an investment ceiling above which they could not rise, thus precluding any significant advantage. Also there was a price floor below which they couldn't fall, thus preventing any possibility of fighting on price.

Faced with this dilemma, P&G conducted some research. This revealed a distinction between the Always consumer and those loyal to mass-market brands. It revolved around a difference between progressive and traditional. The latter group was drawn to what they saw as natural products and tended to view Always as "technologically plasticky". The thicker pads which the mass-market products used had a plus in that they used cotton in the top sheets. This conveyed naturalness and tradition, and the softness of the pads had strong associations with femininity.

This research revealed the latent strength of the whole soft pads category which had always been present, only no one had spotted it. The nature of the pads reflected the traditional women's preference for things natural and feminine. It remained for Procter and Gamble to claim this territory of "Natural Feminine Care" for themselves, underlined by the name "Naturella" which they adopted for the brand. This was a unique position in the category and avoided the rational battleground of "value and reliability" or "technological protection".

The ground that Naturella occupied transcended the traditional topography of the market which had been portrayed as a rational domain where periods were portrayed as a problem, menstruation being just another bodily function. However the traditional women to whom Naturella appealed saw it as a part of the "gift of fertility", a common euphemism for periods being "Mother Nature's gift". Nature was seen as a timeless, sensual and beautiful place – a powerful metaphor for protection. Following on from this, the "Naturella World of Protection" was seen as somewhere women could celebrate "what it meant to be a woman".

In countries as diverse as Mexico, Venezuela, Russia and Poland, this capitalising by Naturella on a generic emotional property led to a rise in volume share from 24 per cent to 40 per cent in just three years. The predicted rate of cannibalisation from the Always brand, based on its market share, would have been around 22 per cent. Yet such was the distinctiveness of Naturella's position that it took only 15 per cent. All this was achieved despite Naturella having a 5.2 per cent price premium against competitive thick pads.[137]

Naturella resolved a personal problem while Aeroguard in Australia combated something which was up close and personal – mosquitoes. It was market leader with a 51.5 per cent value share, but it was declining slightly, by around 1 per cent a year. They needed to target all outdoor Australians who wanted a "mossie-shield". All that was available to Aeroguard was the generic category property of efficacy, so they had to find an engaging way of defining it as unique to Aeroguard. This they did with the concept of a "comfort zone" around an Aeroguard user, where they would be free of annoyance or bother. The comfort for the brand was immediate; over the first three months of the "pest season" value share shot up from 51.5 per cent to 57.6 per cent and volume rose from 49.3 per cent to 54.5 per cent.[138]

Sweet memories

While Aeroguard prospered by promising protection against annoyance, Ving Tours in Sweden prospered by laying claim to the pleasure people found in the memories of their holiday. It was Scandinavia's largest travel company, with 30 per cent of the market. But this size left it vulnerable to its next biggest competitor, as its rational point of difference as Scandinavia's largest company for charter holidays with high perceived quality and good value for money had become a given and had no dynamic emotional appeal. This led Ving to highlight that, with their holidays, the quality was such that "the feeling lasts longer" after the holidaymaker returned home. This distinctive emotional approach leapfrogged over their rational strengths and recovered the lead they had lost to their main competitor through the claiming of this differentiator.[139]

Selling thin air

While Ving had claimed the afterglow of a holiday as their territory, Ford captured thin air when launching the Galaxy MPV. They noticed that empty space was valued by people because it made them feel important and special. The Galaxy was regarded as having a lot of empty space, in common with other MPVs. So Ford translated the luxury of empty space to the proposition of "travel first class".

This resulted in a notable upgrade in sales from the initial launch objective, which had been to beat the sales of the Renault Espace which, at the time, accounted for half the market. The Espace's sales had been running at 7,500 units, whereas the Galaxy dwarfed them with 16,656 units. In addition, Volkswagen launched an almost identical car to the Galaxy, made on the same production line in Portugal, called the Sharan. This only achieved sales of 5,575 units. The power of the Galaxy position in the UK was underlined when the Galaxy was launched at the same time as the Sharan in Germany and France. Taking the average sales of the Galaxy in these two countries as a base for the level of sales in the UK, it was exceeded by 9,197 units.[140]

For those with a bold streak and a little imagination, there is the challenge of successfully charging an additional premium on a product whose market is already a premium category. Champagne is an icon of luxury and its price reflects this, yet Lanson was able to take this further in the UK. Like many of the other products there is a ceiling to the output of champagne. This was due to nearly all the available land in the champagne area being under the vine. Consequently the only way to increase turnover was through higher prices, rather than increased volume.

Most champagnes did not advertise, having long been in a sellers' market. Lanson found a position which focused on the brand and made it personal to the consumer. It was presented as being for people to create their own "Champagne Moment". This reflected the special occasion aspect of champagne and was in fact generic to the product category any brand could have claimed, but only Lanson did.

Over five years Lanson outperformed the market by 32 per cent. Market shipments improved by 92 per cent, whereas Lanson rose by 124 per cent. In addition this was achieved with an increase in prices of 10 per cent against the market. As a result, turnover was £10 million above the projected value.[141]

Scarcity as differentiation

"Tom had discovered a great law of human action, namely, that in order to make a man covet a thing it is only necessary to make the thing difficult to attain", is how Mark Twain summed up the importance scarcity plays in differentiating to produce value. Many years later this was put into practice by Regine, a famous French night club owner. Her original club was in Monte Carlo, where it had become successful and fashionable. She then decided to open a club in Paris. There was so much buzz that everyone wanted to go. But for the first three nights they were met at the door by Regine, who announced that it was already full. In fact it was empty. Subsequent success was guaranteed, and she went on to open clubs around the world.

More recently, Robert Cialdini, in his book *Pre-Suasion* cited a news item he had seen on his local TV news channel on the morning of the release of the latest iPhone. The woman at number twenty-three in the queue revealed that she had been at number twenty-five and had struck up a conversation with the woman at number twenty-three. The latter admired her $2,800 Louis Vuitton shoulder bag. She saw her opportunity and traded the bag for the other woman's place, moving up two places. The news reporter was dumbfounded, but the new number twenty-three explained, "I heard that this store didn't have a big supply, and I didn't want to risk losing the chance to get one."[142] Loss is the ultimate fear which scarcity implies, but it also raises the judged value of that item.

Lacoste, known for its tennis shirts, started selling them in the United States in the 1950s. They became a fashion rage. General Mills acquired the brand in 1969, and it continued to sell well. However, in the mid-1980s, General Mills lowered the price on the shirts and broadened distribution to include discount outlets instead of adding high-end stores. The short-term effect was predictable: sales increased. Yet the brand went from elite stores' racks to clearance bins and lost its cachet. Lacoste repurchased the brand in 1992. It then re-established an element of scarcity by limiting distribution to higher-quality clothing retailers, advertised the brand through celebrities, and raised prices. A change in leadership in 2002 precipitated an even stronger brand focus. Sales jumped 800 per cent.[143]

The scarcity principle is particularly persuasive if a piece of information is found which we think we can't find elsewhere. In an experiment a beef importer gave three different messages to different customers. One was simply asking them to buy. The other was a statement that there was likely to be scarce supplies in the next few months. And finally this last piece of communication was couched in terms of the fact that the information on scarcity was not generally available and came from exclusive contacts. The simple scarcity story sold twice as much as the basic request. But the inside information framing led to sales that were six times the basic request.[144]

When speaking of scarcity, Cialdini made a nice distinction: "knowing the causes and workings of scarcity pressures may not be sufficient to protect us from them because knowing is a cognitive thing and cognitive processes are suppressed by our emotional reactions to scarcity."[145] In an experiment with cookies, the scarce cookies were rated as significantly more desirable, but they were not rated as being better tasting than the abundant cookies. This led him to conclude that "the joy is not in experiencing a scarce commodity, but in possessing it".[146] In other words, this is a differentiation through emotional as opposed to physical satisfaction.

Hermès is a well-established luxury brand which has recognised that its differentiation rests in it always remaining faithful to its roots and the traditions of a small family-run business. Patrick Thomas, the first CEO of Hermès, not to be part of the Dumas family, was clear about their strategy of differentiation through scarcity: "When one of our products sells too much, we discontinue it."[147]

8   The audacity of simplicity

A mistress of Picasso went to visit Matisse when he was too old to paint and so had developed his style of cutouts. When she saw this work she described it as "the audacity of simplicity". On a more prosaic level, there is the admiration for the greatest footballers for doing the simple things well, whereas other, lesser players sometimes have a tendency to showboat. Often they get caught up in intricate crossovers which look accomplished but sometimes confuse even themselves – so too with many of the Brahmins of marketing.

There is little doubt that a cloud of complexity often has a tendency to add a spurious depth to any discussion, whereas it should be the just the opposite. On the top of the brochure for the Apple II was a quote which Steve Jobs was particularly fond of and which is attributed to Leonardo da Vinci: "simplicity is the ultimate sophistication."[148] An example of this in action is Lincoln's Gettysburg address. One of the supreme orators of the day, Edward Everett, was chosen to give the speech dedicating the graveyard. He took several months to prepare it, and in the style of the time, it lasted more than two hours. Lincoln, by contrast, wrote his at the last minute and it only consisted of 250 words and took around two minutes. Yet it is this which has become one of the most iconic speeches in American history, felt to sum up the very essence of the United States. Interestingly part of its initial success was its physical brevity, as the only form of quick communication at the time was the telegraph and it was sufficiently concise to be transmitted and printed by newspapers throughout the country. It went viral.

Simplicity is also important in terms of how much is offered, less can be more when it comes to persuasion. Behavioural scientists Kimberlee Weaver, Stephen Garcia and Norbert Schwarz noticed that people tend to believe that extra features and information will strengthen persuasion. But they felt that rather than providing *additional* benefits the extras actually provided an *averaging* effect. In the same way as when warm water is added to hot water you end up with a more moderate temperature, sometimes adding extra features to an already strong proposal can lead to an actual reduction in its overall attractiveness.

In research they had participants take either the role of presenter or purchaser. The former were provided with two MP3 packages, one was an iPod with a choice of covers; the other was the same offer but with a free music download. The presenters were then asked to say which they felt was the most valuable, and the purchasers were to report how much they would be willing to pay for each. The great majority of the presenters (92 per cent) chose the package with the free download. But the purchasers stated they would pay *less* for this than when no free download was offered. The offer appeared to have cheapened the package.[149] This was also underwritten in another piece of research.

Such an averaging effect can also be noted in a lessening of strategic focus. Often research will reveal a variety of factors which are felt to influence consumer choice. Inevitably an individual brand will be weak on some and, hopefully, stronger on the area where it has chosen to position itself. There is always the temptation to attempt to address these areas of relative disadvantage. This is folly, as the averaging effect comes into play and the resonance of the area where the brand has established a clear point of difference can only be diluted, and the brand ends up with no clear point of differentiation. It is always best to stick to the foundation on which the brand has been positioned and not to try to cover all bases. If anything, the best course is to reinforce the area chosen. Otherwise the inevitable result of a lack of focus is a loss of differentiation.

A similar outcome was also evident in terms of verbal persuasion. In one study respondents received a request to donate to the Make-A-Wish Foundation that had two egoistic reasons for giving – two altruistic ones or all four reasons combined.[150] Giving intentions were much lower in the group provided with four reasons to donate. The explanation for this was that people tended to see the message more starkly as an attempt to persuade them, as the number of reasons increased this heightened resistance. There is a fine balance that needs to be observed, so that overload is avoided and simplicity maintained. Yet there are still legions of advertisements which are often little more than a litany of benefits. Focus would seem to be a wiser route.

Often, in the face of complexity, the simple tends to be discounted and the arcane is lauded. Yet a regard for simplicity should never allow it to become an end in itself as Einstein commented: "everything should be made as simple as possible, but no simpler." There is an irony in the fact that the less people grasp a discourse, the more they tend to be impressed by it. The supreme example of this was the financial crisis of 2008, when most people believed what they acknowledged they did not understand. Much debate on marketing occupies a similar world where the beliefs which often appear to rule seem similar to those of Dorothy regarding the Wizard of Oz. Unfortunately the curtain is seldom pulled back.

Teaching of marketing

The basis for any understanding of a subject is founded in the way it is taught. This is equally valid for marketing, and the narrow way in which it has often been approached from the academic perspective has leached over into discussion of it in the business world. The development of a mechanistic approach in business studies and marketing started around 50 years ago when the Ford and the Carnegie Foundations each commissioned a study of US business education. They concluded that the quality of scholarship was dreadful and suggested that business schools hire people trained in traditional academic disciplines that emphasised quantitative methods like economics, statistics and operations research.

These recommendations were largely adopted and have remained in place until today, symbolised by the increasing obsession with business schools providing qualifications emanating from the academic bubble as opposed to the market in which business operates. This imbalance has resulted in faculty members who have little experience in the real world and tend to rely on the quantitative methods and mathematical models that lend themselves better to academic analysis. A lot of the change has been due to economists, whose influence still dominates, as they were felt to bring the necessary academic rigour. The end result of this is an approach which is prescriptive and didactic rather than descriptive and evidence-based. As Laurence Freedman commented, the nature of economists is that "they showed little interest either in adapting to other disciplines or even worrying about real-world applications".[151] Such a bias provides the foundation for an observation of Kahneman in the related field of social science that "economists have a mystique among social scientists because they know mathematics. They are quite good at explaining what has happened after it has happened, but rarely before."[152] Taken from another angle, economics Nobel Prize winner Robert Shiller stated that "the easiest way to give an economics lecture is once you know the diagrams". Another hassle-free approach to teaching a course he felt is "to mathematise it. First of all, I'll lose 80 per cent of the class. But they can't complain on marks as (the easy answer to them is) there's a 'clear mathematical model answer and you didn't get it.'"[153] If only many in marketing could be as self-aware and honest regarding the tricks they can play, but then this would imply transparency and being opaque is a powerful strategy when wanting to add to one's personal value. As John Locke said in *On the Abuse of Words*, "untruth being unacceptable to the mind of man, there is no other defence left for absurdity than obscurity."

The academics in marketing with a mathematical and theoretical approach far outnumber those who emphasise qualitative techniques and inductive approaches. The former has not only become the template of the approach to marketing in the academic sphere but has also crept into the practical and pragmatic world of business. The result has been a mistaken tendency to employ these theories in the real world, leading to their metamorphosis into practice, which has little empirical justification. This negates the organic nature of the market and undermines the more constructive and effective outcome that can be provided by a holistic and balanced perspective that includes qualitative and inductive approaches. Many are subject to what John Dewey, the American philosopher and psychologist, called "the empiricist's fallacy, which assumes that the parts are prior to the whole when in fact it is the whole that makes the parts what they are".[154] Arthur Koestler looked at it differently when he observed that

> throughout the dark ages of psychology, most of the work done in the laboratories consisted in analysing bricks and mortar in the hope that, by patient effort, somehow one day it would tell you what a cathedral would look like.[155]

Jung helped articulate the dangers inherent in this approach when he observed that scientific education is based, in the main, on statistical truths and abstract knowledge and therefore imparts an unrealistic, rational picture of the world in which the individual, as a merely marginal phenomenon, plays no role. The individual, however, as a rational datum, is the true and authentic carrier of reality, the concrete man as opposed to the unreal ideal or normal man to whom the scientific statements refer.

He went on to observe that "our basic convictions have become increasingly rationalistic. Our philosophy is no longer a way of life, as it was in antiquity; it has turned into an exclusively intellectual and academic affair."[156] It does not take much of a leap to appreciate the relevance of these observations with regard to the approach adopted for marketing.

An illustration of the continued dominance of this mindset was provided by an advertisement for a Research Fellowship in Marketing at Imperial College, London, for the strategic evaluation of brand marketing. The requirement was for someone "to conduct quantitative research on marketing". The objective of this would be "developing a new quantitative model of brand value, identifying key brand building factors and thereby analysing what marketing changes will have the greatest impact on brand value". This is notable for the absence of any mention of the qualitative and inductive approaches, which can help ascertain the emotional dynamics which, as has been discussed, are an essential part of a brand's make-up. In design terms this would be called a triumph of form over function; in this case it appears as a victory of process over results. A brand and the market in which it operates is organic; the logical outcome of the mechanistic requirements of this brief from Imperial College would appear to be a model of a robot.

The limitations of the robotic model have been realised by those who try to develop artificial intelligence (AI). As Duncan Watts noted, they

> realised that the list of potentially relevant facts and rules is staggeringly long. In fact it is generally impossible to know in advance which things can be ignored and which cannot. So they had to widely over-programme their creations in order to perform even the most trivial tasks.[157]

This is a good illustration of the daunting complexity that confronts anyone trying to achieve a mechanistic interpretation of what is an organic process.

It is also worth noting that the objective of the Imperial College project was a recent obsession – that of brand value. This is a valuable concept, as it is helpful to have some estimate of how much a brand is worth when the company which owns it is being bought. In some respects it is like the "good will" which has a monetary value put on it when a going concern, such as a restaurant, is bought. But this latter example is real in that an actual purchase is being considered, and it is a value that is agreed on by both sides, whereas brand value is merely an estimate which has, at its core, subjective evaluations – hence the large differences between the values produced by the different companies specialising in this field. Value is what buyers are prepared to pay for something and cannot be realistically established until that crucial moment of purchase intent arrives. The fallacy of valuations having a subjective base is well illustrated by the fact that Apple was valued at $3 million in 1978 by venture capitalists. Yet by the end of 1980, less than a month after its initial public offering, when people were establishing a real value through the shares they bought, it had a stock market value of $1.8 billion.[158] Despite this reality, it is disturbing to see how the conjecture which is inherent in brand valuations has become regarded as fact, as brands are now quoted as actually having the specific values which are estimated, and there are even league tables which are regularly produced of which individual brands are stated as being worth more than others, rather like a hit parade. The difference is that the latter is built on actual sales, whereas the core of brand value is no more than musings.

Meretricious metrics

Following on from such hollow metrics, Roger Martin of the Rotman Business School in Toronto gave a proper background when he wrote, "the great weakness of the quantitative approach is that it takes the context out of human behaviour, removing an event from its real-world setting and ignoring the effects of variables not included in the model."[159] A fellow Canadian, Henry Mintzberg, gave further perspective when he said that "starting from the premise that we can't measure what matters gives managers the best chance of realistically facing up to their challenge."[160] This is reminiscent of the observation by the Chinese philosopher Laotse that "thirty spokes meet the axle, but it is the space between them which is the true nature of the wheel. Vessels are made from clay, but it is the space within which is their true nature." A more recent observation was that of the American surgeon Atul Gawande who remarked on how the measurable replaces the important.[161]

Unfortunately many in marketing have not heeded the truth of these observations and continue to weave webs of greater complexity as a supposed aid to the subject, basing them on metrics which purport to measure the degree of differentiation. But their main accomplishment is to make it more opaque. One trope is to quantify concepts which cannot submit to such metrics, and then put forward propositions based on these measurements. In effect, these are built on foundations of sand. As Hilary Austen, in her book *Artistry Unleashed*, observed, "qualities cannot be objectively measured, as a quantity like temperature can be measured. We can count the number of people in a room but that tells us little about the mood – upbeat, flat, contentious or the group's interaction."[162]

Often such exercises are clear illustrations of confirmation bias, which Richard Thaler described as "a natural tendency to search for confirming rather than disconfirming evidence".[163] They are seduced by a process described by the strategist Igor Ansoff when "corporate managers start off trying to manage what they want and finish up wanting what they can measure".[164] Even though the validity of some measurements is dubious, it is enough that they have been proposed, as they give a spurious impression of certainty. A standard approach is the invention of a measure which then, unsurprisingly, is a key component in justifying a particular proposition. This activity is no more pronounced than in the multiple ways in which it is claimed that emotions can be measured. These attempts to rationalise emotions are, in effect, an oxymoron; they are like trying to nail custard to a wall. As the neurologist Joseph Le Doux, author of *The Emotional Brain*, stated, "one of the most significant things ever said about emotion is that everyone knows what it is until they are asked to define it."[165] He went on to describe emotions as "mental states that fall outside the domain of cognitive explanation".[166] Le Doux commented on how preferences can be formed without any conscious registration of the stimuli, and at the end of the day, emotions have primacy over cognition.

Unfortunately the failure to accept what appears to be only common sense has led to an avalanche of arcane and meretricious metrics. It appears to be akin to inventing new cards at a game of poker and then discovering how many can be dealt and enthusiastically endorsed. The bluff never seems to be called, the poker face of plausibility is seldom questioned. Robert McNamara, Secretary of Defence under Kennedy and a highly successful director of Ford, recognised only later in life that he had focused on what could be measured, rather than what needed to be understood.

One measure which comes from the intellectualisation of marketing is Lovemarks,[167] which was trumpeted as an idea centred on emotions to replace that of brands. Kevin Roberts, the originator of this term, claimed that "Brands are running out of juice". He felt that love was needed to rescue brands. Roberts asked, "What builds loyalty that goes beyond reason? What makes a truly great love stand out?" As usual, Roberts employed the familiar trope of inventing a new paradigm for which he conveniently had the answer. Rather than brands running out of juice, it appeared that it was rather Roberts's understanding of them which had run out and he wanted a new model. In familiar fashion he then went on to make this concept even more complicated by suggesting that his invention was made up of "mystery", "sensuality" and "intimacy", subscribing to a frequent measure of the weight of a concept which tends to be its degree of complexity. In this he is a clear example of the lack of awareness and failure to consider the foundations of marketing mentioned earlier. He could have been confused by the fact that most definitions of a brand are merely descriptions, but if he had cared to look a little further he might have discovered one of the clearest definitions is that people buy products for their *functional* benefits, whereas they buy brands for their *emotional* benefits. Bill Bernbach, one of the founders of the advertising agency Doyle Dane Bernbach, said, "You can say the right thing about a product and nobody will listen. You've got to say it in such a way that people feel it in their gut. Because if they don't feel it, nothing will happen."[168] Both these observations pre-empted Roberts by several decades and have the simplicity and directness which his poker card sadly lacks. But then, repackaging an idea and presenting it as a revelation is a familiar trick in many fields as well as marketing.

The origins of Lovemarks are provided by the fact that the publisher, powerHouse Books, named Saatchi & Saatchi as one of its corporate partners, stating it was "here to help your brand bring its story into print and reach its audience". This self-promotion did pay off, as Lovemarks itself was established as a brand, and in September 2006, Saatchi & Saatchi, of which Roberts was the CEO, won the $430 million J. C. Penney account and the idea of Lovemarks was said to be instrumental in this.

While swinging around in the forest canopy with J. C. Penney, sight of grounded reality appeared to have been lost, as with so many similar meretricious metrics. If only half as much effort could be put into consideration of the simple fundamentals, such as the definitions of marketing and of a brand, then there would be an agreed basis for discussion, and a clearing might be found in this dense undergrowth of complexity. And maybe a little light might then be permitted to get through.

Not content with just single dimensions, sometimes a whole new eco structure is assembled, such as in the case of a Brand Experience Index,[169] which was invented by a "creative" agency called Rufus Leonard. This is also a good example of how the media which comments on marketing accepts these poker hands without ever inspecting the cards. *Marketing Week*, a prominent magazine in the UK, had a headline for this topic of "Marketers that fail to address brand experience will see loyalty drop". In another article it explained how "a new study has identified 'four pillars of great customer experience' on which marketers should concentrate their efforts".[170] These were presented as though they were the hard currency of thought that had been unearthed, rather than mere suggestions. Such bombast dressed as profound insights into a supposed reality is the usual way of reporting similar topics, putting them forward as something which is already accepted rather than the simple hypotheses which they in fact are. A hypothesis needs to be subjected to a certain amount of rigour in order to establish its worth; this seems to be absent. In the light of so many supposed certainties, it is no wonder that those involved in marketing so often have difficulty in seeing the wood for the trees.

In the case of the Brand Experience Index, the agency had claimed to identify five core facets of brand experience that have a direct impact on customer loyalty. These included "think", which refers to a brand's ability to communicate its purpose; "sense", where a brand engages customers through the five senses using immersive experiences; "feel", which involves creating emotional impact; "do", whereby a brand facilitates behaviours and solves problems for consumers; and "connect", which involves inspiring a sense of belonging. To construct the index, research was conducted in which respondents were asked to rate brands according to the five facets, which presumably they had never heard of before, using a seven-point scale.

Not content with this, the study also incorporated a partnership with brand valuation consultancy Brand Finance that they felt was aimed at exploring the effect of the index on the bottom-line value of a brand, thus helping further embed it as a credible metric. Although Rufus Leonard stated that this cross-analysis is at an early stage, it claimed to have found a correlation between its index scores and the brand value of low-cost airlines. "[Brand Finance] postulates that a one-point increase in [the Brand Experience Index] score could lead to a business value increase of as much as $99m (£74m) in the case of Ryanair," the report said. With a web of such complexity, no doubt this spider would catch a few flies. At least it has a role in being a nice illustration of Armstrong's Seer-Sucker theory, as well as Levitt's description of "shamans in business suits".

Margaret Heffernan noticed a trait with sociologists and economists that "until they have, in a word, rationalised the behaviour they do not feel that they have really understood it".[171] But the reality is different for, as Leonard Mlodinow observed, "our sensory perceptions, our memory recall, our everyday decisions, judgements and activities all seem effortless – but that is only because the effort they demand is expended mainly in parts of the brain that function outside awareness."[172]

The paramount position of emotions

In marketing this has led to what appears to be an ongoing sore in terms of discussion – the supposed separation between the rational and emotional. The pre-eminence of the former has been largely discounted by Kahneman in his scepticism with regard to the rational model of thinking, and it is also implicit in his distinction of thinking between System 1 and System 2 referenced previously. In terms of marketing, it is important to note his description of System 1 as "effortlessly originating impressions and feelings that are the main sources of the explicit beliefs and deliberate choices of System 2".[173] As marketers' main concern is with beliefs and choices, it is curious why they have not viewed reason with a proper perspective and have continued to give it a significance it does not appear to merit, often lauding it over emotions.

Also the power of emotions was given added perspective by Le Doux when he observed that

> the fact that emotions, attitudes, goals and the like are activated automatically (without any conscious effort) means that their presence in the mind and their influences on thoughts are not questioned. They are trusted the way we would trust any other kind of perception.[174]

He went on to comment that we don't consciously understand the basis of an emotional appraisal, as we don't necessarily have access to the emotional processes: "most likely, attempts to find an all-purpose emotion system have failed because such as system does not exist."[175] Yet those in marketing still try to apply reason to emotions, a clear case of using something that is not fit for purpose.

The predominant role of System 1 thinking in marketing was summed up by Alexander Segart, the managing director of Goal, a Swiss PR company which had great success in Swiss political advertising: "we're successful because we know how to reduce information to the lowest level, so people respond to it without thinking." On a wider plane is the response of Adlai Stevenson, who was twice a presidential candidate in the 1950s. An enthusiastic supporter said he had the support of every thinking American. "Thank you madam," he replied, "but I need to win." Seen in this light, the limited role of System 2 thinking in choice is apparent, yet the vacuous debate persists between reason and emotion, with little reason for the former other than the facility of presenting it as plausible. It seems that few in marketing have heeded the observation of Pascal that "the heart has many reasons of which reason knows nothing".

Le Doux pointed out that the mind is traditionally viewed as a trilogy of cognition, emotion and motivation. He observed that "thinking and related cognitive processes were (and for the most part still are) emphasised at the expense of emotion and motivation . . . Thinking cannot be fully comprehended if emotions and motivations are ignored".[176] He went on to define emotions as "the process by which the brain determines or computes the value of stimulus"[177] and pointed out how emotions amplify memories. At its most profound, "attention, perception, memory, decision-making and the conscious concomitants of each are all swayed in emotional states. The reason for this is simple: emotional arousal organises and coordinates brain activity."[178] He concludes, "that emotions are powerful motivators seems indisputable."

On a more prosaic level there is the example of the action replay in sport, particularly football. The effect of this is to slow down the action and make it appear as though a particular move was considered rather than merely an immediate reaction to the situation, in many cases just instinctive. In the same way the rational conceit tries to slow down by analysis the decision process of the individual and so present the outcome as the result of the conscious consideration which reason requires in order to be operative and to effectively change the process from System 1 to System 2 thinking.

The insights of Kahneman and the importance of emotions have been echoed in the work of the neurologist Antonio Damasio, who wrote, "emotion is integral to the process of decision-making, for worse or for better."[179] He referred to a study of individuals who were entirely rational in the way they ran their lives up to a time when, as a result of neurological damage in specific sites of their brains, they lost a certain class of emotions and, as a consequence, lost their ability to make rational decisions.[180] As he commented,

> These findings suggest that selective reduction of emotion is at least as prejudicial for rationality as excessive emotion . . . Well-targeted and well-deployed emotion seems to be a support system without which the edifice of reason cannot operate properly.[181]

Donald Norman added greater precision when he stated that "because we are only aware of the reflective level of conscious processing, we tend to believe that all human thought is conscious . . . Cognition tries to make sense of the world, emotion assigns value."[182]

The questioning of reason

The weight given to reason as a differentiator is rather redundant in the face of recent understanding of cognition and, more particularly, the views of Kahneman and Tversky that the rational agent model did not describe humans well. In economics the obsession with rationality had led to the identification of the "Econ" who inhabits a world, described by the Swiss economist Bruno Frey as one where "the agent of economic theory is rational, selfish and his tastes do not change". Kahneman and Tversky identified another group at variance with these creatures which they called "Humans" – a rather refreshing realisation. Kahneman went on to explain it more fully:

> Rationality is logical coherence – reasonable or not. Econs are rational by this definition, but there is overwhelming evidence that Humans cannot be. An Econ would not be susceptible to priming, WYSIATI,[183] narrow framing,[184] the inside view[185] or preference reversal,[186] which Humans cannot consistently avoid.[187]

This has been further developed by Mercier and Sperber, with the contention that the principal function of reasoning is argumentative and that its main contribution is to the effectiveness and reliability of communication, rather than any cognitive or behavioural outcomes, as is often suggested in marketing. They went on further to suggest that when reason is applied to conclusions of intuitive reference, it tends to rationalise them, rather than correct them.[188] Yet often those in marketing insist on giving a rational framework to the behaviour of consumers, when most recent evidence is to the contrary. They forget that reasoning is a conscious process, whereas most of our behaviour appears to be governed by the unconscious, particularly as articulated by System 1 thinking.

It seems that reason can actually interfere with judgements, as our automatic implicit attitudes differ from our consciously controlled explicit attitudes. This is the Dual Attitude System whereby the mental processes that control our social behaviour are distinct from those through which we explain it.[189] The easily verbalised factors are often less important in terms of the actual decisions with which they are associated. Often our gut-level attitudes guide our actions, and then our rational mind makes sense of them.

As neuroscientist Sam Harris commented, "the intention to do one thing and not another does not originate in consciousness – rather it *appears* in consciousness."[190] This was underlined by Michael Gazzaniga, professor of psychology at the University of California: "because consciousness is a slow process, whatever has made it to consciousness has already happened; it is a *fait accompli*."[191] Giving reasons can make unimportant considerations temporarily salient and produce a less, not more, accurate assessment of how we really feel.

As Jonathan Haidt commented, reason is like a government press secretary; it is there to defend your decision to others. Most tellingly, he observed that "anyone who values truth should stop worshipping reason".[192] The moral philosopher Mary Midgley summarised the situation by noting, "In becoming more intelligent we have become more aware, which other creatures aren't. It is not to do with reason."[193] The challenge for marketing is to make greater use of this awareness.

The Dual Attitude System can result in reasoning being an actual hindrance to the making of a decision. Timothy Wilson, a social psychologist at the University of Virginia, found that if participants were first asked to analyse and rationalise their feelings, the gauging of these emotions was undermined. In one study, college students were asked to evaluate five posters. Two were of fine art – Monet and van Gogh – and the other three featured captioned cartoons or photos of animals. Previous testing with students had established that most preferred the Monet and van Gogh. In this experiment, half the students were asked to write a brief essay explaining why they disliked or liked each of the five posters. The other half were just asked to choose.

Those who had to write the essay expressed a preference for the cartoons and photos, whereas those asked just to choose plumbed for the fine art. The participants were then allowed to take home the posters they had chosen. A few weeks later they were contacted. Those who had chosen the cartoons and photos were far less satisfied with their choices. They had been less likely to want to take them home, have them hanging up or even to have kept them. In contrast, those choosing the fine art had largely kept their posters.[194] Wilson did a series of other experiments underwriting these findings. Interestingly, these observations were echoed by the American Pulitzer Prize–winning poet John Ashbery, when he remarked that "the worse your art is, the easier it is to talk about it".[195]

Reason is raised to a pinnacle and enshrined in many rational models such as the Efficient Market Hypothesis, which states that market efficiency causes existing share prices to always incorporate and reflect all relevant information. But one of the most successful investors in the market has been George Soros, whose son observed, "you know the reason he changes his position on the market or whatever is because his back starts killing him. It has nothing to do with reason."[196] There is also the paradox that reason, when practiced by the individual, can be viewed objectively as failing in reason. As Jon Elster pointed out, "reasons are reasons for action when, given the beliefs of the agent, the action in question is the best way to realise his desire".[197] This observation has an ultimate consequence whereby the act of putting pins in a doll to cause another harm can be seen as a rational act by its practitioner, as it is based on his or her beliefs. On a broader canvas, Malcolm Gladwell commented about fundamental judgements, such as liking someone, that "if such judgements are made without thinking, then surely they defy explanation."[198]

There is also the unfortunate truth that scientific discourse sounds more authoritative than social discourse. Those with this perspective would do well to heed the sign in Einstein's office that "not everything that can be counted counts and not everything that counts can be counted". On the contrary, when challenged regarding the scientific approach, its proponents seem unable to digest the arguments against it. They appear to be following the well-known observation of Upton Sinclair that "it is difficult to get a man to understand something when his salary depends upon him not understanding it" – a precautionary observation of which many in marketing could take note.

9 The light which difference brings to marketing

The important point to bear in mind about differentiation is that it helps make choice easier for the consumer, whether at a conscious or, more likely, unconscious level. There is evidence that, in some respects, this is something the consumer welcomes. Despite discussion of the need for choice, it can present the individual with an uncomfortable dilemma. As the Slovenian philosopher and sociologist Renata Salecl observed, choice involves a loss.[199] Janet Landman in her book *Regret* added to this: "the greater the number of appealing choices, the greater the opportunity for regret." In theory it sounds great, as when 65 per cent of people surveyed said that *if* they were to get cancer, then they would want to choose their own treatment. But among people who *actually* had cancer, only 12 per cent wanted to do so.[200] This is another example of the well-documented but often forgotten chasm between reported intentions and actual behaviour. In a study conducted by Yankelovich Partners, quoted by Barry Schwarz in his book *The Paradox of Choice*, a majority of people want more control over their lives, but a majority want to simplify them.[201]

By highlighting a clear and unique difference from its competitors, a brand can help alleviate the dilemma of the consumer to the advantage of both parties. The marketing skill is choosing an aspect which has some resonance with the consumers. All too often it is something which those who manage the brand feel *should* strike a chord, but the sad truth is that it is a hollow note and only has relevance to themselves. Often this is brought about either by their heightened interest in aspects which are irrelevant details to the wider audience of the consumer or their failure to grasp that it is not enough to convey reality but that the only effective form of communication is when perceptions are altered. In addition there is the familiar trope, which has been mentioned, of choosing an extrinsic property to differentiate, which is a false premise. This has an inherent danger, as it provides the competition with the keys to citadel – for unless a clear and solid claim is made, as these elements are outside the brand they can just as easily be picked up by its rivals. Through the use of such properties the most likely outcome is that, if both sides play with them, then they both lose out because the differentiation might be in the mind of the marketers, but this tends to self-delusion, as it is seldom picked up by the consumer. The greatest of these dangers is the extrinsic property of price and the false promise of discounting, when brands can easily enter a downward spiral.

The greatest irony in relation to differentiation is that it is so simple and basic that few give it the proper recognition and position it deserves. Instead there is a tendency to climb higher and higher in ivory towers which, however enchanting and intriguing, can have little solidity without the foundation which differentiation provides. It is the DNA of marketing, a brand would not exist without it, yet it is seldom accorded this status.

This is not to deny that there is a great deal of thought devoted to marketing. But this seems to be often focused on spinning webs of increasing complexity which become ends in themselves, whereas the most fundamental and basic task should be to establish the essence of the marketing which describes and informs the canvas on which all subsequent thought should take place. The fact that there is no real definition of marketing, nor apparent interest in arriving at one in the sense of something which sums up its essence, is a searing indictment of how far the discipline has strayed from its roots. The consequences of this are only too apparent in the profusion of hypotheses, many of which are backed up by meretricious metrics. Yet all of these are blindly accepted as having a validity which might be real but has seldom any empirical basis. They have become the currency of marketing without the underpinning of a central bank.

There is supreme irony in the tendency of many supposed experts in marketing feeling that they have the solid certainty of a scientific basis for it, as the American theoretical physicist Richard Feynman said, "science is the belief in the ignorance of experts."[202] He felt that science was about embracing doubt – being open to the possibility, even likelihood that your theory was wrong. The British military historian, Sir Michael Howard, echoed this when he observed of his own field that "history which challenges the comfortable assumptions and providential narratives of a shared group identity may be painful, but it is also a sign of maturity and wisdom".[203] Although marketing is a much younger discipline, there is no reason why it also should not aspire to these qualities. So far it seems to be failing.

What is most unfortunate is that marketing is a business tool which can be almost magical in its effect, as evidenced by the difference made by simply changing the name Pilchards to Cornish Sardines. Frustratingly for many, it is considered an arcane art, even among members of the business community, as has been shown by the blinkered attitude of some within the wine industry. Even Sir Stuart Rose, the former head of Marks and Spencer, who was attributed with turning the company around, stated that "I have never wanted to use the word 'strategy' to describe what we've done because that makes it sound terribly complicated and it's not".[204] But this is a basic misunderstanding of strategy as it is only valid if everyone can march to its tune. If it is complicated, then it has failed in its purpose. Like the understanding of the word "marketing", this failure to grasp what strategy means shows the ignorance of the basics which undermines marketing. In this case the associations which had built up around the word "strategy" had produced this blinkered negative reaction, even from one so august. For many there is a similar reaction to "marketing".

How much of this is due to the way that marketing is taught, with its continued emphasis on the rational choice model, or to the "shamans in business suits" described by Levitt? It is up to the individual to decide. Because of its undoubted value, marketing has been progressively detached from its core to a degree which allows self-appointed experts to thrive and, above all, profit. Hopefully the focus on the basic building block of difference will help dispel some of these cobwebs and focus on the essence of marketing, bringing its magic to the fore.

Notes

Introduction

1 Theodore Levitt, "Marketing Myopia", *Harvard Business Review* (July–August 1960): 43–60
2 Duncan J. Watts, *Everything Is Obvious, Once You Know the Answer*, Atlantic Books, 2011, p. 28
3 S.J. Gould, *New York Review of Books*, 26 June, 1997
4 Marshall's Nobel Prize acceptance speech, "*Helicobacter* Connections", http://www.nobelprize.org/nobel_prizes/medecine/laureates/2005/marshall-lectiure.pdf
5 Eric Fromm, *The Sane Society*, Routledge, p. 14
6 Daniel Kahneman, *Thinking, Fast and Slow*, Allen Lane, 2011, p. 217
7 "Today", *BBC Radio 4*, 26 September, 2014
8 S. Armstrong, "Evidence-Based Advertising: An Application to Persuasion", *International Journal of Advertising*, 30, No. 5 (2011): 743–767
9 Richard Thaler, *Misbehaving*, Allen Lane, 2015, p. 270
10 James Surowiecki, *The Wisdom of Crowds*, Little Brown, 2004
11 Theodore Levitt, *The Marketing Imagination*, The Free Press, 1983
12 Margaret Heffernan, *Wilful Blindness*, Simon and Schuster, 2011, p. 239
13 Robert B. Zajonc, "Attitudinal Effects of Mere Exposure", *Journal of Personality and Social Psychology*, 9 (1968): 1–27
14 S. Armstrong, "Evidence-Based Advertising: An Application to Persuasion", *International Journal of Advertising*, 30, No. 5 (2011): 743–767
15 J.B. Engelmann, C.M. Capra, C. Noussair and G.S. Berns, "Expert Financial Advice Neurobiologically 'Offloads' Financial Decision-Making Under Risk", *PLoS One*, 4 (2009), No. 3: e4957. doi:10.1371/journal.pone.0004957
16 John Dewey, Jo Ann Boydston and Paul Kurtz, *The Later Works of John Dewey 1925–53*, SIU Press, 2008, p. 5
17 Robert B. Cialdini, Noah J. Goldstein and Steve J. Martin, *The Small BIG – Small Changes That Spark Big Influences*, Profile Books, 2014, p. 6
18 *Ibid.*, p. 7
19 John Locke, *Of the Abuse of Language*, Penguin, 2009 (first published 1690)
20 "The Commoditization of Brands and Its Implications for Marketers", *Copernicus and Market Facts*, December 2000
21 Bruce Springsteen, *Born to Run*, Simon and Schuster, 2016

Chapter 1: Context

22 Noah J. Goldstein, Steve J. Martin and Robert Cialdini, *The Small BIG*, Profile Books, 2014, p. 6
23 "This Much I Know," *Observer*, 30 July, 2006
24 D.C. Blanchard and R.J. Blanchard, "Crouching as an Index of Fear," *Journal of Comparative Physiological Psychology* (March 1969) 67(3): 370–375
25 Kaufer and Francis, "Nurture, Nature and the Stress that Is Life". In M.Brockman (ed), *Future Science: Essays from the Cutting Edge*, Vintage, 2011, pp. 56–71
26 easyJet plc, results for six months ended 10 March, 2016
27 "Marketing 'More Important Than Ever' Post-Brexit Says EasyJet", *Marketing Week*, 19 September, 2016
28 Adrian C. North, David J. Hargreaves and Jennifer McKendrick, "In-Store Music Affects Product Choice", *Nature*, 390 (13 November, 1997): 132
29 Jeremy King, "Changing Tastes in Restaurant Design", *Financial Times*, 31 January, 2015
30 Dan Ariely, *Predictably Irrational*, Harper Collins, 2008, pp. 4–6
31 Itamar Simonson, "Get Closer to Your Customers by Understanding How They Make Choices", *California Management Review* (1993) 35(4): 68–84
32 *Consumer Reports*, January 1975, p. 62
33 "Starbucks' staff set to get free shares in incentive scheme", *Observer*, 12 December, 2010
34 Future Foundation, May 2004
35 Michael J. Newcombe and Neal M. Ashkanasy, "The Role of Affective Congruence in Perceptions of Leaders: An Experimental Study", *Leadership Quarterly*, 13, No. 5 (2002): 601–604
36 S.T. Fiske and S.E. Taylor, *Social Cognition*, Reading, MA: Addison-Wesley Pub. Co., 1984
37 Walter Isaacson, *Steve Jobs*, Little, Brown, 2012, p. 320
38 "Apple Tops Retail Charts", *RetailSale/24/7 Wall Street/Seeking Alpha*, Warc, 28 February, 2012
39 "15 Second Ads Reign Supreme on US TV", *New York Times*, Warc, 1 November, 2010
40 Leonard M. Lodish and Carl F. Mela, "If Brands Are Built Over Years, Why Are They Managed Over Quarters", *Harvard Business Review* (July–August 2007): 104–112

Chapter 2: The intrinsic

41 "Jeanette Winterson: All about my Mother", *The Guardian*, 29 October, 2011
42 Walter Isaacson, *Steve Jobs*, Little, Brown, 2012, p. 328
43 *Financial Times*, Warc, 31 August, 2011
44 http://www.brigitte.de/service/presse/mitteilungen/marken-erfolgreicher-als-prominente-1128366/
45 Ingvar Kamprad, "A Furniture Dealer's Testament", quoted in Bertil Torekull, *Leading by Design: The IKEA Story*, HarperCollins, 1999, p. 228
46 *The Times*, 9 June, 2011
47 Leonard M. Lodish and Carl F. Mela, "If Brands Are Built Over Years, Why Are They Managed Over Quarters", *Harvard Business Review* (July–August 2007): 104–112
48 Richard Thaler and Cass Sunstein, *Nudge*, Penguin, 2009, p. 4
49 Arthur Conan Doyle, *The Boscombe Valley Mystery*, *The Strand Magazine*, 1891

50 "A Life Scientific", *BBC Radio 4*, 25 March, 2015
51 David Robinson and Bill Breen, *Brick by Brick*, Random House Business Books, 2013, p. 288
52 Jonathan Cahill, *Igniting the Brand*, Marshall Cavendish, 1998
53 "How Advertising Helped Saab Take Off", *IPA Effectiveness Awards*, 1988
54 Billetts, Warc, 16 October, 2008
55 Walter Isaacson, *Steve Jobs*, Little, Brown, 2012, p. 347
56 Susan Boyle, "This Much I Know", *Observer*, 9 December, 2012
57 *Ibid.*, p. 324

Chapter 3: Telling a unique story

58 Julian Baggini, *The Ego Trick*, Granta, 2011, p. 85
59 Nichols Epley, *Mindwise*, Allen Lane, 2014, p. 126
60 Daniel Kahneman, "The Thought Father", *London Evening Standard*, 18 March, 2014
61 Michael Lewis, *The Undoing Project: A Friendship that Changed the World*, Allen Lane 2017, p. 250
62 Lucy Kellaway, *Sense of Nonsense in the Office*, London: FT/Prentice Hall, 2000, p. 19
63 Joseph Le Doux, *The Emotional Brain*, Phoenix, 1998, p. 57
64 Kenneth Roman, "Jack Daniel's: The Illusion of Discovery". https://www.thedrinks business.com/2016/10/jack-daniels-the-illusion-of-discovery/
65 "Alexander Keith's", Institute of Communications Agencies, Canada, 2005
66 http://significantobjects.com/about
67 Dan Ariely, *Predictably Irrational*, Harper Collins, 2008, pp. 4–6
68 Jimboingo, "The Wicked Sick Project – BMX", http://www.youtube.com/watch?v=Grnew7dqrhk
69 David Robertson and Bill Breen, *Brick by Brick*, Random House, 2013, p. 205
70 http://www.farrow-ball.com/colours/paint/fcp-category/list
71 "The Food Programme", *BBC Radio 4*, 28 August, 2016
72 "Bowmore: Shifting the Balance of Power", *IPA Effectiveness Awards*, 2000
73 "Glenmorangie: 'It's Quiet. Too Quiet.' Glenmorangie Quietly Confounds the Market", *IPA Effectiveness Awards*, 2000
74 Sascha Topolinski and Rolf Reber, "Gaining Insight Into the 'Aha' Experience", *Current Directions in Psychological Science*, 19, No. 6 (2010): 402–405
75 Maryanne Wolf, *Proust and the Squid*, Cambridge: Ikon Books, 2008, p. 90
76 Robert McKee, *Story*, Methuen, 1999
77 *Ibid.*
78 "The Secret of Film Success", *The Times*, 13 August, 2011

Chapter 4: It's not reality that needs to be different, but perceptions

79 Daniel Kahneman, "The Thought Father", *Evening Standard*, 18 March, 2014
80 Donald A. Norman, *The Design of Everyday Things*, MIT Press, 2013, p. 59
81 "Hurricanes With Female Names Kill More People, Study Finds", *Time*, 2 June, 2014
82 Robin Goldstein and Alexis Herschkowitsch, *The Wine Trials*, Fearless Critic Media, 2008
83 Debanjan Mitra and Peter N. Golder, "Quality Is in the Eye of the Beholder", *Harvard Business Review* (April 2007): 26–27
84 Walter Isaacson, *Steve Jobs*, Little, Brown, 2012, p. 392

85 *Ibid.*, p. 393
86 Walter Isaacson, *Steve Jobs*, Little, Brown, 2012, p. 467
87 Daniel Kahneman, *Thinking, Fast and Slow*, Allen Lane, 2011, p. 20
88 *Ibid.*, p. 21
89 Richard A. Thaler, *Misbehaving*, Allen Lane, 2015, p. 121
90 "Stella Artois: Reassuringly Expensive", *IPA Effectiveness Awards*, 1992

Chapter 5: The power behind words

91 Iain McGilchrist, *The Master and His Emissary: The Divided Brain and the Making of the Western World*, Yale University Press, 2009, p. 228
92 Leonard Mlodinow, *Subliminal: The New Unconscious and What It Teaches Us*, Penguin, 2012, p. 64
93 Isaiah Berlin, *Russian Thinkers*, Penguin, 1994, p. 209
94 "The Fall of a Corporate Queen", *Economist*, 5 February, 2005
95 *Ibid.*
96 Robert Cialdini, *The Psychology of Persuasion*, Harper Collins, 2007, p. 4
97 N. Guéguen and L. Lamy, "The Effect of the Word 'Love' on Compliance to a Request for Humanitarian Aid: An Evaluation in a Field Setting", *Social Influence*, 6, No. 4 (2011): 249–258, doi:1080/15534510.2011.627771
98 C.R. Crichter and T. Gilovich, "Incidental Environmental Anchors", *Journal of Behavioural Decision Making*, 21 (2008): 241–251
99 David Jago of Mintel on "The Food Chain", *BBC World Service*, 27 August, 2016
100 "New HTC CMO Scraps 'Ask the Internet' Campaign, Returns to Robert Downey Jr.", *Advertising Age*, 9 March, 2015
101 "Ten-Fold Leap for HTC Smartphones and People Still Prefer Apple", *Forbes Asia*, 19 April, 2016
102 "Desert Island Discs", *BBC Radio 4*, 8 July, 2016
103 Dan Gardner, *Risk*, McClelland and Stewart, 2008, p. 309
104 Hofling, C. K., Brotzman, E., Dalrymple, S., Graves, N. and Bierce, C., "An Experimental Study of Nurse-Physician Relationship", *Journal of Nervous and Mental Disease*, 143 (1966): 171–180
105 L. Bickman, "The Social Power of a Uniform", *Journal of Applied Social Psychology*, 4 (1974): 47–61
106 Duff McDonald, *The Firm: The Story of McKinsey and Its Secret Influence on American Business*, Simon and Schuster, 2014
107 "Vorsprung durch Technik – ad slogan that changed how we saw Germany", *The Guardian*, 18 September, 2012
108 "Who Are You Calling Pilchard? It's 'Cornish Sardine' to You . . .", *The Independent on Sunday*, 17 August, 2003
109 "Cornish Sardines Given Protected Food Status", *Daily Telegraph*, 11 December, 2009
110 Kahneman, Daniel and Amos Tversky. "On the Psychology of Prediction," *Psychological Review* 80, no.4 (1973): 237-51
111 John Elster, *Sour Grapes: Studies in the Subversion of Rationality*, Cambridge University Press, 1983
112 Max Muller, *The Science of Thought*, London: Longmans Green, 1887, pp. 78–79
113 See "The Simplified: A Conversation With John Bargh", *Edge*, http://www.edge.org/3rd_culture/bargh09/bargh09_index.html
114 Antonio Damasio, *The Feeling of What Happens*, Vintage, 2000, p. 294
115 Tim Lott, "Telling It Like It Is", *Observer*, 11 September, 2016

Chapter 6: Visual differentiation

116 "Why Are 10,000 Children Missing in Europe", *BBC World Service*, 10 October, 2016
117 "A Town, If Not a Painting, Is Restored", *New York Times*, 14 December, 2014
118 Lesley Stahl, *Reporting Live*, Touchstone, 1999
119 Shawn W. Rosenberg, Lisa Bohan, Patrick McCafferty, and Kevin Harris, "The Image and the Vote: The Effect of Candidate Presentation on Voter Preference", *American Journal of Political Science*, 30, No. 1 (February 1986): 118–127
120 Iain McGilchrist, *The Master and His Emissary: The Divided Brain and the Making of the Western World*, Yale University Press, 2009
121 Walter Isaacson, *Steve Jobs*, Little, Brown, 2012, p. 78
122 *Ibid.*, p. 132
123 *Ibid.*, p. 343
124 "How Big Tobacco lost a Crucial Battle for Hearts and Minds", *Observer*, 22 May, 2016
125 Canadian picture warnings: "A Picture Is Worth a Thousand Words", *American Psychological Association Monitor*, June 2001, p. 14
126 Norbert Schwarz, Hyunjin Song, and Jing Xu "When Thinking Is Difficult: Metacognitive Experiences as Information", in *Social Psychology of Consumer Behavior*, ed. Michaela Wanke, New York Psychology Press, 2009, pp. 201–223
127 Donald A. Norman, *The Design of Everyday Things*, MIT Press, 2013, p. 3
128 R.G. Heath, "Reassuringly Expensive – a Case History of the Stella Artois Press Campaign", in *Advertising Works 7*, ed. C. Baker, Henley-on-Thames: NTC Publications, 1993
129 Donald A. Norman, *The Design of Everyday Things*, MIT Press, 2013, p. 3, 184

Chapter 7: Differentiation comes in many forms

130 Theodore Levitt, *The Marketing Imagination*, The Free Press, 1983
131 *Ibid.*
132 Laurence Freedman, *Strategy*, Oxford University Press, 2013, p. 479–485
133 "Purolator", Institute of Communications Agencies, Canada, 1995
134 https://www.ocado.com/webshop/product/Napolina-Bronze-Die-Linguine/298784011
135 Robert McKee, *Story*, Methuen, 1999
136 "Batchelors Supernoodles: Leading From the Front", *IPA Effectiveness Awards*, 1998
137 "Naturella – Mother Nature's Gift: How Communications Drove One of the Most Successful Launches in One of the Most Challenging Marketplaces in the World", *IPA Effectiveness Awards*, 2006
138 "Aeroguard – Your Force Field Against Mossies", *IPA Effectiveness Awards*, 2002
139 "Ving Tours", *Euro Effie Awards*, European Association of Communications Agencies, 1999
140 "Ford Galaxy: Building Brand Value for Ford", *IPA Effectiveness Awards*, 1998
141 "Champagne Lanson: Why Not?" *IPA Effectiveness Awards*, 1994
142 Robert Cialdini, *Pre-Suasion*, Random House, 2016, p. 167
143 Leonard M. Lodish and Carl F. Mela, "If Brands Are Built Over Years, Why Are They Managed Over Quarters", *Harvard Business Review*, (July/August 2007): p. 104–112

144 A. Knishinsky, "The Effects of Scarcity of Material and Exclusivity of Information on Individual Buyers Perceived Risks in Provoking a Purchasing Decision", Doctorate Dissertation, Arizona State University, 1982
145 Robert Cialdini, *The Psychology of Persuasion*, Harper Collins, 2007, p. 266
146 *Ibid.*, p. 266
147 Paul Simonet and Carlos Virgile, "Luxury Brand Marketing: The Art of Luxury", *Admap*, November 2013

Chapter 8: The audacity of simplicity

148 Walter Isaacson, *Steve Jobs*, Little, Brown, 2012, p. 80
149 Kimberlee Weaver, Stephen M. Garcia, and Norbert Schwarz, "The Presenter's Paradox", *Journal of Consumer Research*, Vol. 39, No. 3 (October 2012), pp. 445–460
150 D.C. Feiller, L.P. Tost and A.M. Grant, "Mixed Reasons, Missed Givings: The Costs of blending Egoistic and Altruistic Reasons in Donation Requests", *Journal of Experimental Social Psychology*, 48, No. 6 (2004): 1322–1328
151 Laurence Freedman, *Strategy*, Oxford University Press, 2013, p. 517
152 Kahneman, "This Much I Know", *The Observer*, 8 July, 2012
153 Robert Shiller, talk at the Royal Society of Arts, 12 November, 2015
154 John Dewey, "The Reflex Arc Concept in Psychology", in Jo Ann Boydston (ed.) *The Early Works*, Vol. 5, Southern Illinois University Press, 1972, p. 99
155 Arthur Koestler, *The Ghost in the Machine*, Hutchinson, 1967, p. 19
156 Carl Jung, *The Undiscovered Self*, English Edition, Routledge and Kegan Paul, 1958, p. 52
157 Duncan Watts, *Everything Is Obvious, Once You Know the Answer*, London: Atlantic Books, 2011, p. 4
158 Cynthia Montgomery, *The Strategist*, Collins, 2012, p. 112
159 Hilary Austen, *Artistry Unleashed: A Guide to Pursuing Great Performance in Work and Life*, University of Toronto Press, 2010
160 "Measurement", *Observer*, 10 February, 2008
161 Atul Gawande, "Reith Lectures", *BBC Radio 4*, 25 November, 2014
162 Hilary Austen, *Artistry Unleashed*, University of Toronto Press, 2010
163 Richard Thaler, *Misbehaving*, Allen Lane, 2015, p. 172
164 "Measurement", *Observer*, 10 February, 2008
165 Joseph Le Doux, *The Emotional Brain*, Phoenix, 1998, p. 23
166 *Ibid.*, p. 35
167 Kevin Roberts, *Lovemarks: The Future Beyond Brands*, PowerHouse Books, 2004
168 W. Bernbach, "Facts Are Not Enough", *Proceedings of the Annual Meeting of the American Association of Advertising Agencies*, White Sulphur Springs, West Virginia, 14–17 May, 1980
169 "Marketers That Fail to Address Brand Experience Will See Loyalty Drop", *Marketing Week*, 7 September, 2016
170 "The Four Pillars of CX", *Warcnews*, 14 September, 2016
171 Margaret Heffernan, *Wilful Blindness*, London: Simon & Schuster, 2011, p. 37
172 Leonard Mlodinow, *Subliminal: The New Unconscious and What It Teaches Us*, Penguin, 2012, p. 34
173 *Ibid.*, p. 21
174 Joseph Le Doux, *The Emotional Brain*, Phoenix, 1998, p. 63
175 *Ibid.*, p. 106

176   Joseph Le Doux, *Synaptic Self*, Penguin, 2003, p. 174
177   *Ibid.*, p. 206
178   *Ibid.*, p. 225
179   A. Damasio, *The Feeling of What Happens*, Vintage, 2000, p. 41
180   A. Bechara, A. Damasio, H. Damasio and S. Anderson, "Insensitivity to Future Consequences Following Damage to Human Prefrontal Cortex", *Cognitum*, 50 (1994): 7–15
181   *Ibid.*, p. 42
182   Donald A. Norman, *The Design of Everyday Things*, MIT Press, 2013, p. 47
183   What You See Is All There Is. Participants who saw one side of an argument being more confident of their judgements than those who saw both sides. Knowing little makes it easier to fit everything you know into a coherent pattern.
184   The difference between being told to make a decision as if it was the only one and a broad framing when it was treated as one of many. The latter blunted the emotional reaction to losses and increased the willingness to take risks.
185   People who have information about an individual case rarely feel the need to know the statistics of the class to which the case belongs.
186   The moral intuitions that come to your mind in different situations are not internally consistent.
187   Daniel Kahneman, *Thinking, Fast and Slow*, Allen Lane, 2011, p. 411
188   Hugo Mercier and Dan Sperber, "Why Do Humans Reason? Arguments for an Argumentative Theory", *Behavioral and Brain Sciences*, 34 (2011): 57–111
189   Timothy Wilson, Samuel Lindsay and Tonya Schooler, "A Model of Dual Attitudes", *Psychological Review*, 107 (2000): 101–126
190   Sam Harris, *Free Will*, Free Press, 2012, p. 8
191   Michael Gazzaniga, *Who's in Charge?* Ecco, 2011, p. 124
192   Jonathan Haidt, *The Righteous Mind: Why Good People are Divided by Politics and Religion*, Allen Lane, 2012
193   Mary Midgley, *The Solitary Self: Darwin and the Selfish Gene*, Acumen Publishing, 2010
194   T.D. Wilson, D.J. Lisle, J.W. Schooler, S.D. Hodges, D.J. Klaarne and S.J. Fleur, "Introspecting About Reasons Can Reduce Pre-Choice Satisfaction", *Personal and Social Psychology Bulletin*, 19 (1993): 331–339
195   Quoted by Adam Phillips in *Missing Out, In Praise of the Unlived Life*, Penguin, 2013, p. 44
196   Malcolm Gladwell, *What the Dog Saw*, Little, Brown and Company, 2009
197   John Elser, *Sour Grapes: Studies in the Subversion of Reality*, Cambridge University Press, 1983
198   *Ibid.*

Chapter 9: The light which difference brings to marketing

199   Renata Salecl, *The Tyranny of Choice*, Profile Books, 2011
200   Barry Schwarz, *The Paradox of Choice*, Ecco paperback, 2005, p. 32
201   *Ibid.*, p. 25
202   Richard Feynman, *The Meaning of It All: Thoughts of a Citizen-Scientist*, lectures originally given in 1963
203   M. MacMillan, *Dangerous Games: The Uses and Abuses of History*, New York: The Modern Library, 2009, p. 39
204   Stuart Rose, "Back in Fashion", *Harvard Business Review*, 85, No. 5 (May 2007): 51–58

Index

For Product Safety Concerns and Information please contact our EU
representative GPSR@taylorandfrancis.com
Taylor & Francis Verlag GmbH, Kaufingerstraße 24, 80331 München, Germany